A CLOSER LOOK
DECEPTIONS AND
DISCOVERIES

Marjorie E. Wieseman

NATIONAL GALLERY COMPANY, LONDON
DISTRIBUTED BY YALE UNIVERSITY PRESS

Marjorie E. Wieseman is Curator of Dutch Painting at the
National Gallery, London. Her publications include *Dutch Painting*
(National Gallery Company, 2007). and *Vermeer's Women: Secrets
and Silence* (Yale University Press, 2011)

A Closer Look: Deceptions and Discoveries is published to accompany the
exhibition *Close Examination: Fakes, Mistakes and Discoveries*, held at the
National Gallery, London, from 28th June to 12th September 2010.
This exhibition is supported by the Engineering and Physical
Sciences Research Council.

Front cover, half-title and title page: Caspar David Friedrich (1774–1840),
Winter Landscape, probably 1811, detail of painting and infrared reflectogram.
Pages 4–5: Detail of Luca Giordano, *A Homage to Velázquez*, about 1692–1700.
Pages 34–5: Detail of Lorenzo Lotto, *Portrait of a Woman inspired by Lucretia*,
about 1530–2.

10 9 8 7 6 5 4

First published 2010 by National Gallery Company Limited
St Vincent House, 30 Orange Street, London WC2H 7HH
www.nationalgallery.co.uk
ISBN 978185709 486 2
1018545

British Library Cataloguing-in-Publication Data
A catalogue record is available from the British Library
Library of Congress Catalog Card Number: 20099347850

PROJECT EDITOR Claire Young
EDITOR Catherine Bradley
DESIGNER Bianca Ng
COVER ARTWORK Smith and Gilmour
PICTURE RESEARCHER Suzanne Bosman
PRODUCTION Jane Hyne and Penny Le Tissier
COLOUR REPRODUCTIONS DL Repro Ltd
Printed and bound in Hong Kong by Printing Express

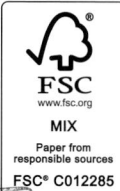

FSC
www.fsc.org
MIX
Paper from
responsible sources
FSC® C012285

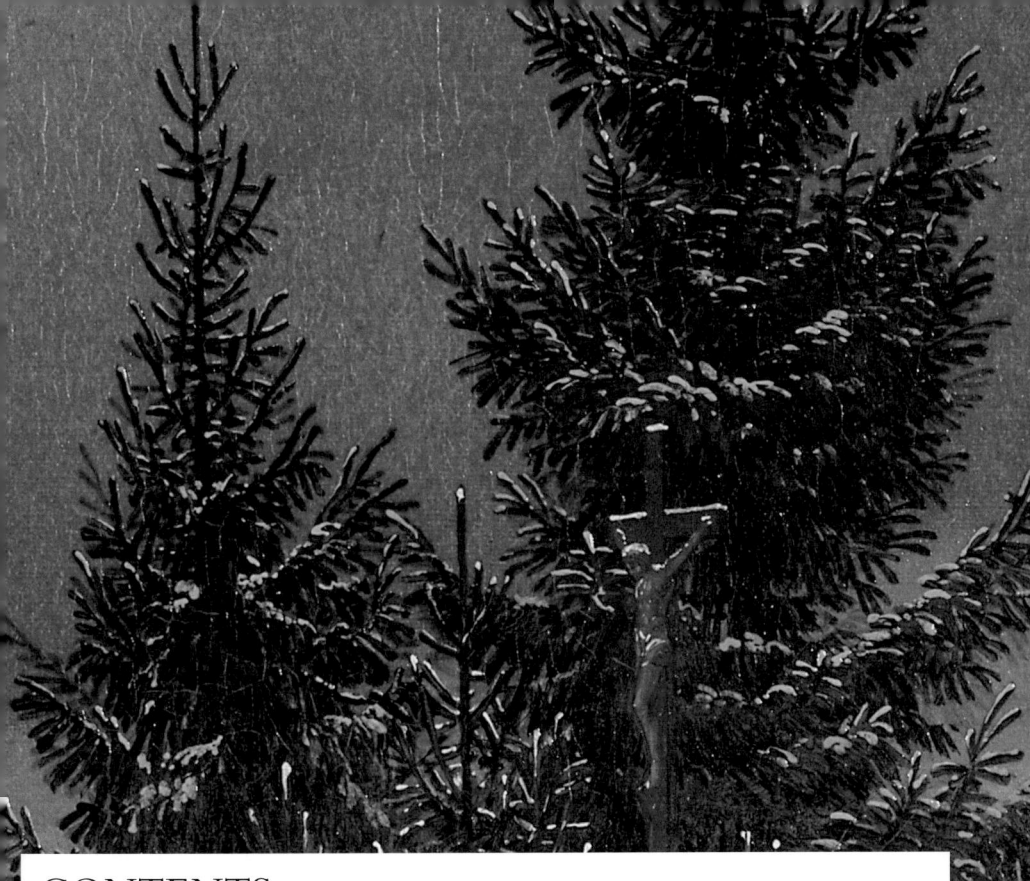

CONTENTS

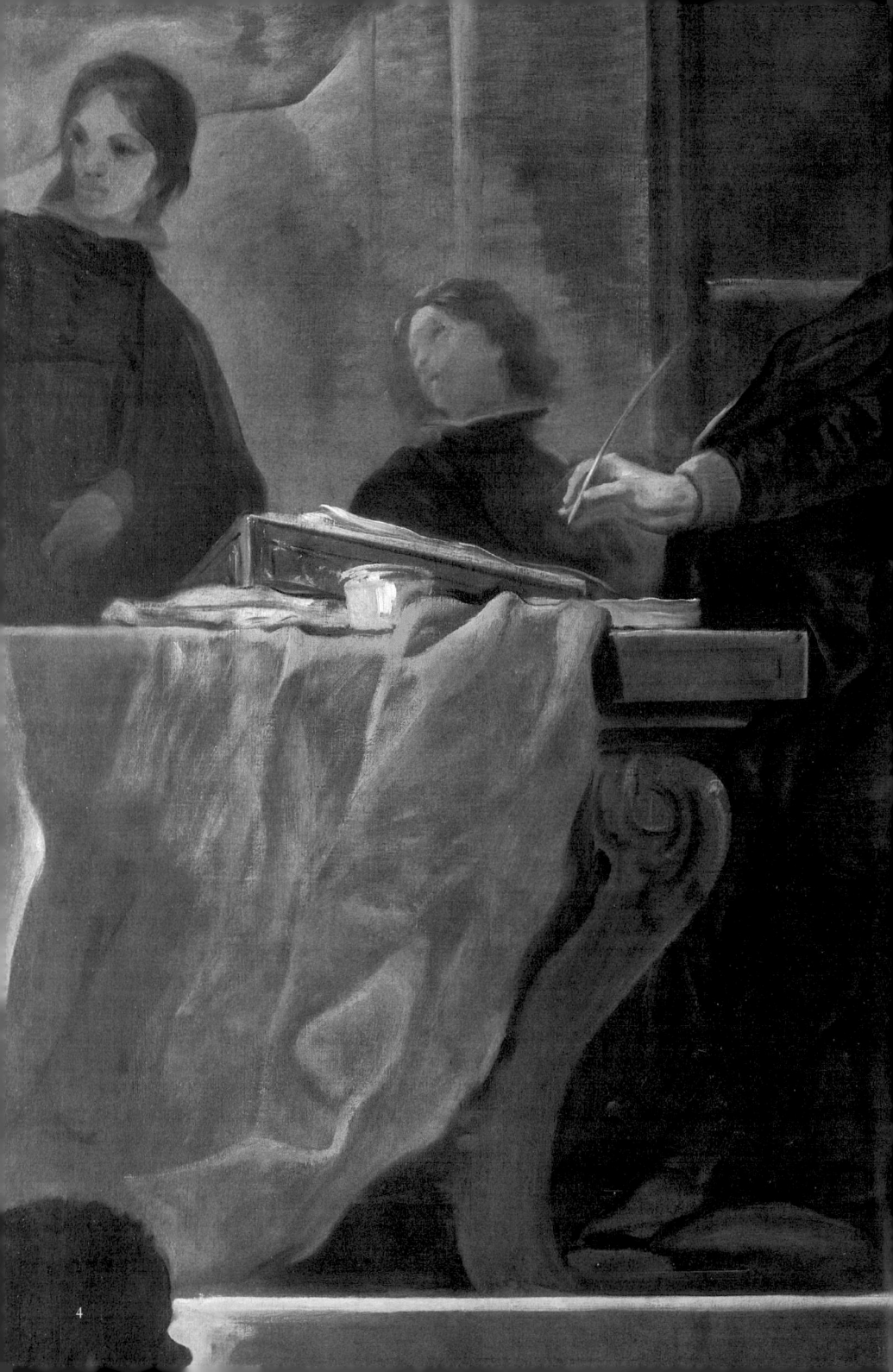

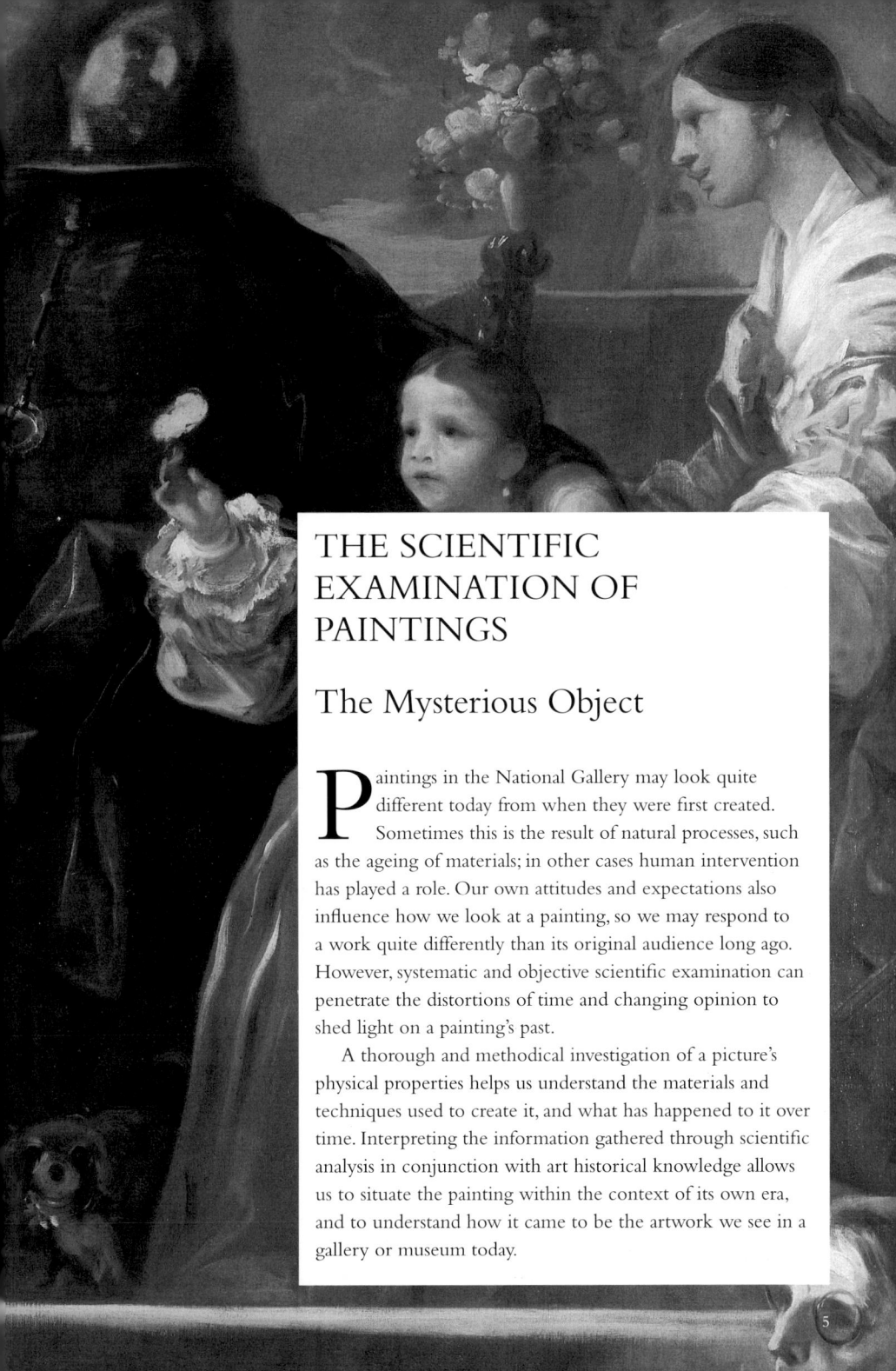

THE SCIENTIFIC EXAMINATION OF PAINTINGS

The Mysterious Object

Paintings in the National Gallery may look quite different today from when they were first created. Sometimes this is the result of natural processes, such as the ageing of materials; in other cases human intervention has played a role. Our own attitudes and expectations also influence how we look at a painting, so we may respond to a work quite differently than its original audience long ago. However, systematic and objective scientific examination can penetrate the distortions of time and changing opinion to shed light on a painting's past.

A thorough and methodical investigation of a picture's physical properties helps us understand the materials and techniques used to create it, and what has happened to it over time. Interpreting the information gathered through scientific analysis in conjunction with art historical knowledge allows us to situate the painting within the context of its own era, and to understand how it came to be the artwork we see in a gallery or museum today.

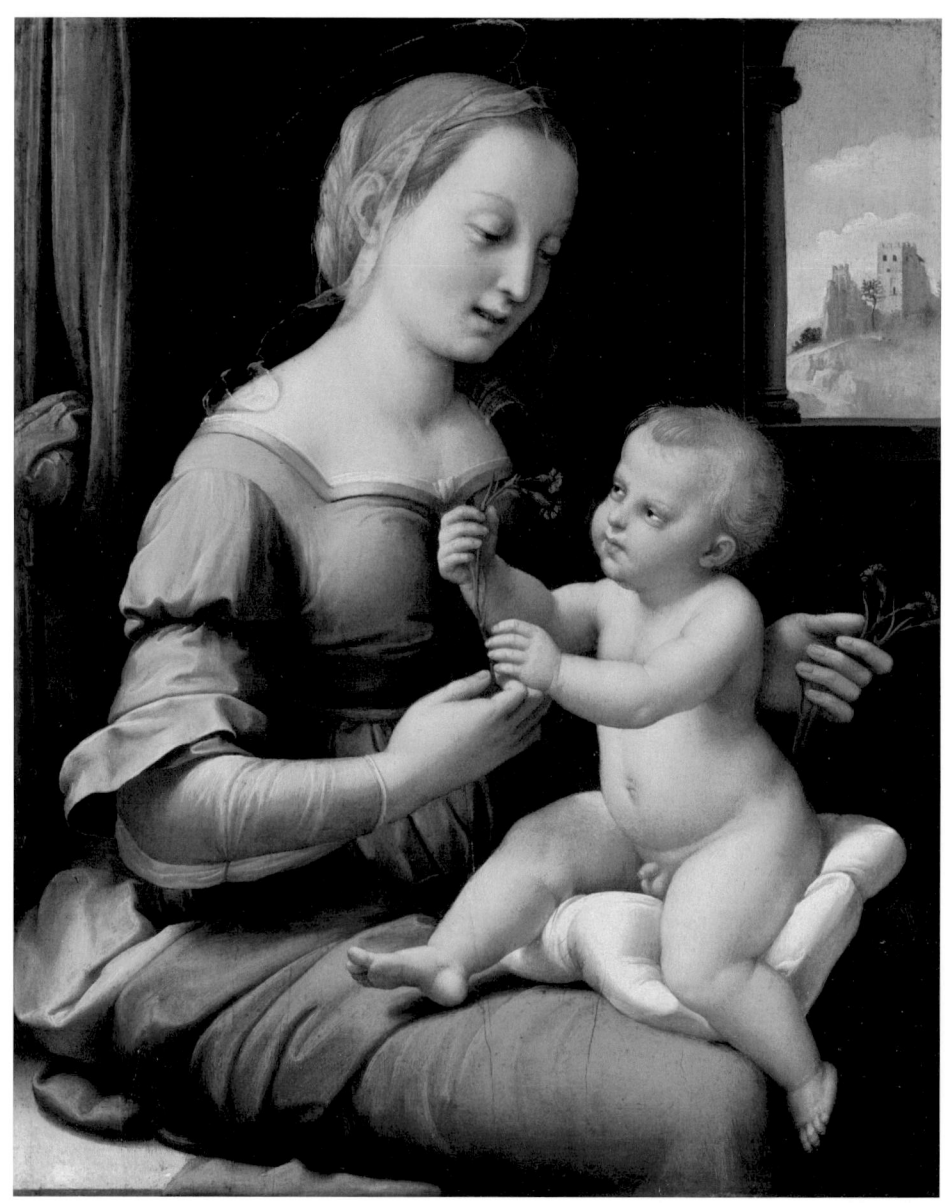

1. Raphael (1483–1520), *Madonna of the
Pinks ('La Madonna dei Garofani')*,
about 1506–7, oil on yew, 27.9 x 22.4 cm.
For more than a century this painting
was considered merely a copy, but in 1991
a combined scientific and art historical
investigation proved it was an original
painting by Raphael (see p. 88).

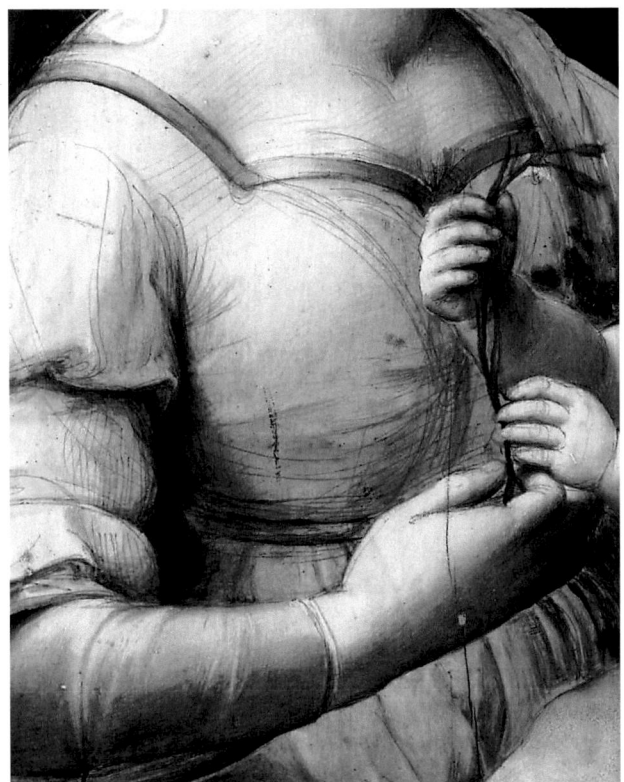

Technical research (the investigation of a painting's physical properties) draws on the combined skills of scientists, restorers, curators and art historians; it takes place in laboratories, studios, libraries, archives and many other, less expected places. Sometimes the most profound discoveries happen instantaneously, but more often it takes years of slow, painstaking research to arrive at the solution to a puzzle. Technical research is a constantly evolving process of detection and discovery, flexible enough to accommodate the unique set of problems and conditions that each painting presents. For example, a centuries-old painting might have been damaged, or its materials may have degraded, or its appearance been altered during its creation, whether by the artist or by a later hand. The painting may have been attributed to different artists over time, each shift reflecting advances in scholarship or changes in taste. Using a broad range of investigative and analytical techniques (terms marked in **bold** are defined in a glossary on pages 92–3), technical examination can identify physical changes to an object and explain the reasons for them. It can give insight into the artistic practice of a local or national school or period and identify traits specific to an individual artist or workshop. It can also disclose information about the past owners of a particular work. Objective scientific examination can also balance historical assessments driven by a desire to recognise great works by iconic artists. It thus complements **connoisseurship** – the ability to make reasoned assessments about artistic authorship, to distinguish between originals and copies, and to identify forgeries. Finally, a thorough understanding of the methods and materials used in the production of paintings is essential for deciding a safe and effective approach to conservation treatment.

Although scientific examination can deliver information about paintings that cannot be determined otherwise, it inevitably has limitations. For example, while analysis can show whether a painting's material characteristics are reasonably consistent with a proposed attribution, it cannot establish a positive relationship between artwork and artist. It can only effectively eliminate paintings which, based on clearly defined scientific facts, cannot have been produced during the active lifetime of the artist in question. As noted above, scientific examination does not replace traditional connoisseurship and art historical research, but it is an extraordinarily powerful tool when used in concert with them. Close collaboration between scientists, curators and restorers has been a cornerstone of research at the National Gallery for many decades. Results of their investigations are published regularly in the *National Gallery Technical Bulletin*, and a number of examples are featured in the case studies included in this book.

The value of science in the study and conservation of paintings was recognised as long ago as 1850, when concern over the effects of central London's notoriously noxious atmosphere led chemist and physicist Michael Faraday to recommend the appointment of '…a person of competent chemical knowledge and a little acquainted with paintings in ancient and modern times' to study the impact of pollution on the National Gallery's collection. Only in 1934, however, was a Scientific Department established, its initial purpose to advise on safe and appropriate techniques for the proposed cleaning of pictures. While this remains one of the Department's primary functions, its remit has broadened to encompass more general technical research on the collection in support of art historical investigations. Continuing technical research has allowed it to build an ever more refined history of the material practice of painting throughout 750 years of development and change. In addition, the Department is responsible for the research and monitoring of environmental

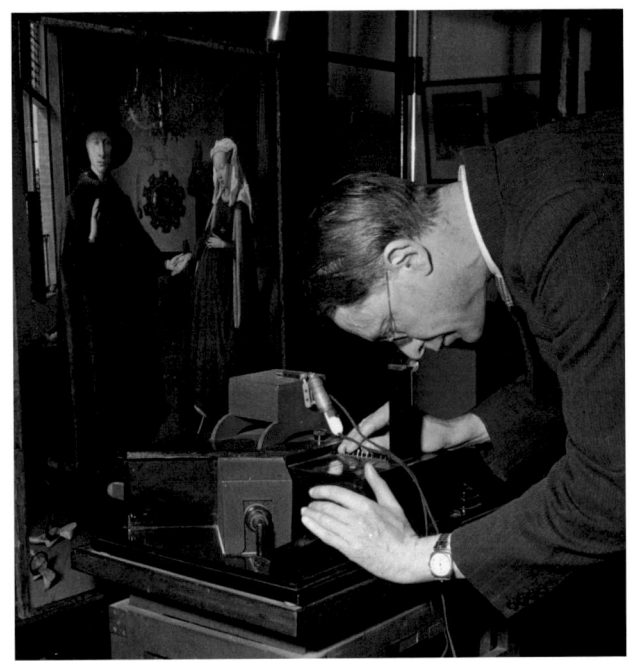

3. The National Gallery established a Scientific Department in 1934. This photograph shows scientific advisor Ian Rawlins measuring colour on *The Arnolfini Portrait* (1434) by Jan van Eyck in 1947.

conditions and their impact on paintings, and with the Conservation and Photographic Departments, for the technical imaging of paintings. Through its many activities, the National Gallery's Scientific Department has become – and remains – a leader in technical research on all aspects of Old Master paintings.

Looking Closely at Paintings

Applying scientific methods to the study of paintings generally progresses from the simplest techniques to more complex, specific analyses. The first step of any technical examination is a study of archival evidence (documents that might provide information about the painting, its manufacture, or earliest owners), together with a thorough visual examination. This furnishes researchers with as much information as possible about a painting's physical condition, how it was made, and the artistic and historical context in which it was created. These findings direct the focus of subsequent scientific investigations. Over many decades National Gallery scientists have built a large and growing database of the material characteristics of paintings in the collection, dating from around 1260 to the early twentieth century. Such information is essential for interpreting the results of new investigations.

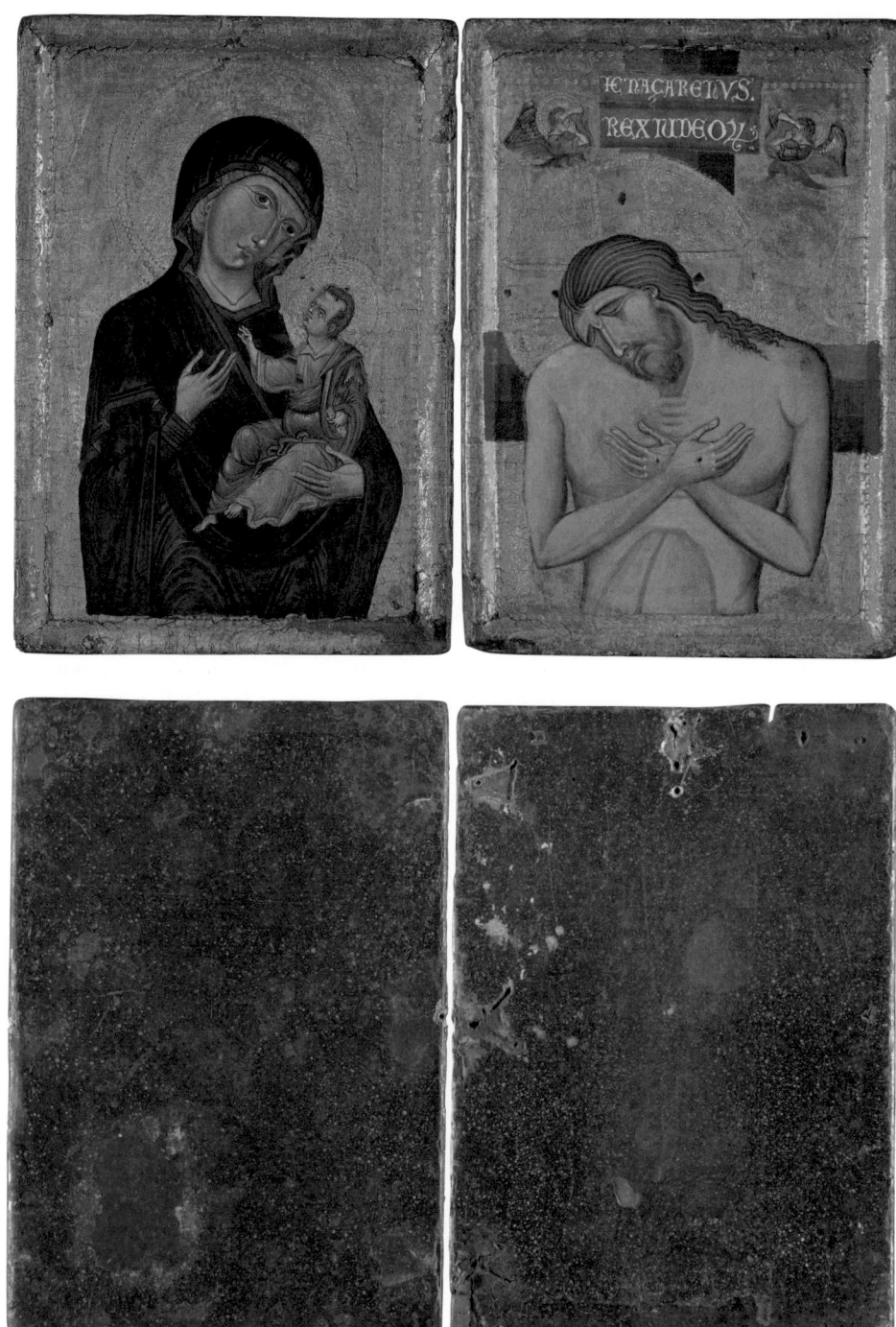

Opposite 4 a and b (above) and 5 a and b (below). Italian, Umbrian, *The Umbrian Diptych* (*The Virgin and Child* and *The Man of Sorrows*), about 1260, egg tempera on wood, 32.4 x 22.8 cm each. The unknown artist of these paintings was probably influenced by Byzantine icons. The small scale of the diptych suggests it was intended for private devotions. On the reverse of these panels the hinge marks are clearly visible, proving that these panels were joined as a pair.

Below left: 6. Microscopic examination of a panel painting.

Below right: 7. Photomicrograph of *Saint Francis before the Sultan*, 1437–44 by Sassetta (active by 1427; died 1450). This detail shows blue pigment over silver leaf. The area shown is approximately 5mm across.

Visual examination might begin by inspecting the painted surface to verify that the appearance, texture and pattern of **craquelure** (the network of fine cracks in the paint surface) are all consistent with the work's proposed age and likely materials. Any apparent anomalies, and any visible areas of damage or repaint, are noted for further investigation. By examining the painting's surface with a stereo binocular microscope (usually around 50× magnification), experts can assess details of brushwork and craquelure. They can study the sequence of paint and ground layers between cracks, and distinguish areas of repaint by observing paint applied over existing cracks in the original aged paint surface. Microscopic examination may also be sufficient to identify certain coarsely ground pigments and pigment mixtures *in situ*, without the need for more invasive techniques (case study 7, 16).

As well as the carefully prepared 'face' of a painting, the back and sides can be especially rich sources of information about a work's construction, original format and function, geographic origin, dating and provenance. When the thirteenth-century Umbrian painting of *The Man of Sorrows* was examined in 1948 [4b], for example, areas of damage at the left side of the panel were recognised as the traces left by three hinges – a sign that the panel had once formed the right wing of a diptych. Some 50 years later a previously unknown painting of the Virgin and Child came to light [4a]. Not only did it exhibit the same characteristic painting style and distinctive punchwork decoration as *The Man of Sorrows*, but it also bore distinctive marks along the right side caused by the removal of metal hinges [5b]. Precisely matching these marks helped to prove that these paintings had once been hinged together. The National Gallery acquired the two pieces in 1999, successfully reuniting the diptych after a long separation.

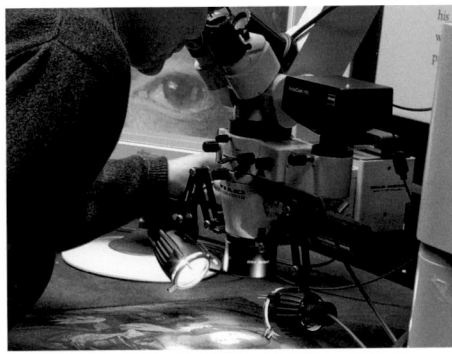

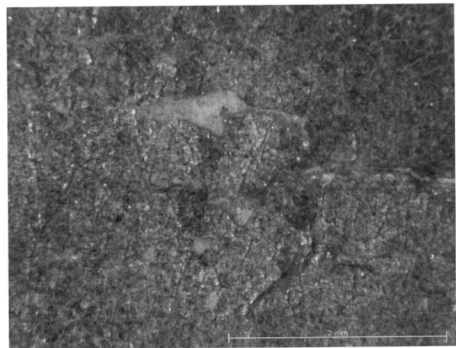

8. German, *Edzard the Great, Count of East Friesland,* eighteenth century, oil on oak, 48.9 x 36.2 cm. This painting was acquired as a work of the sixteenth century, but the results of dendrochronological examination of the oak panel determined that the last growth ring was formed in 1696.

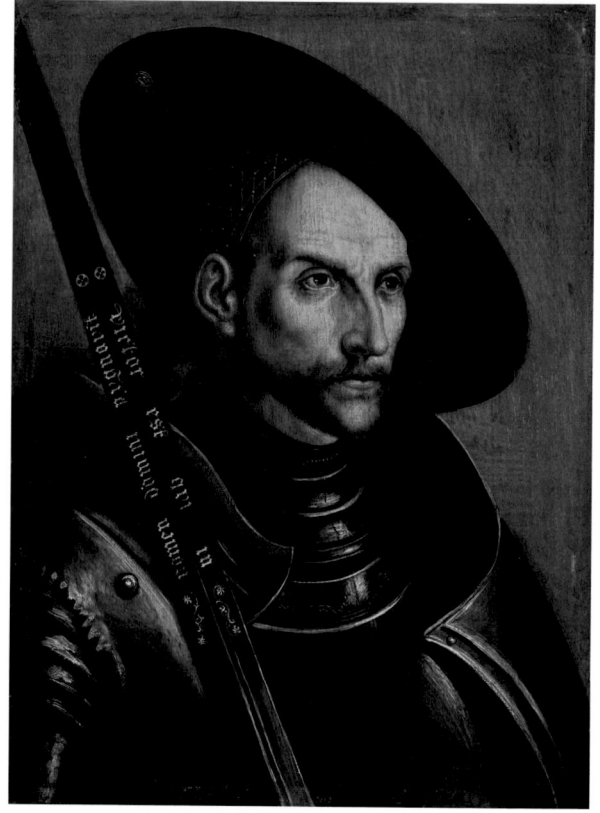

Knowledge of historic techniques can also help experts determine a painting's approximate age and place of origin. Before the eighteenth century, for example, wood panels used for painting were finished by hand; when they survive in their original state, the backs often still exhibit traces of the tools used to work the wood. Later, machine-sawn panels generally have a more uniform appearance. The backs of Italian poplar wood panels were usually left quite rough, while Northern European panels, typically made of closely grained oak, tend to be more finely crafted and neatly finished. Similar distinctions can also be made for canvas supports. As the fabric is inherently vulnerable, however, few canvases, at least of older paintings, have survived without a later reinforcement (lining). This added layer of canvas impairs access to the original fabric.

The wood from which a panel is made can reveal a lot about where and when a picture produced. Visual assessment and microscopic examination of samples can identify the wood type, and experts are sometimes able to approximate a panel's

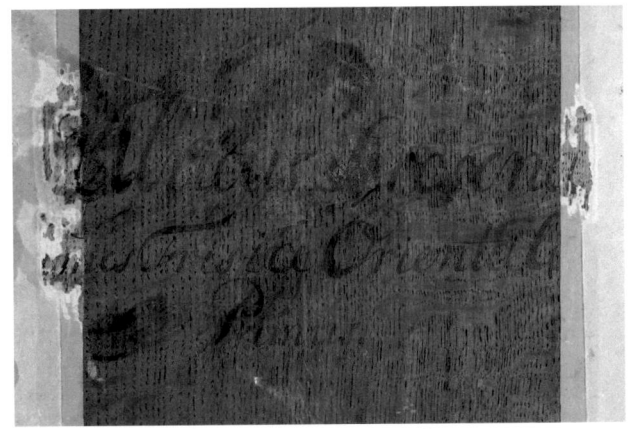

9. The information a painting yields must always be verified. The inscription on the back of the portrait reproduced on the facing page incorrectly identifies the subject as Ulrich Cirksena, First Count of East Friesland. It is actually his son, Edzard, who is depicted.

age through **dendrochronology**. This technique works by measuring growth rings that have formed in the wood over centuries, and comparing them with patterns in a master chronology database. Where the patterns match, it is possible to give a date for the last ring measured on the panel, and so to calculate the wood's age [8].

Dendrochronology works best for woods such as oak, which has clearly identifiable annual growth rings. Unfortunately poplar – the wood most commonly used for Italian panel paintings – does not form regular annual rings, so is unsuitable for dating in this way.

Even with a suitable wood, scientists can usually suggest only approximate dates. A precise date can only be obtained when the tree's bark and most recent growth rings are present, but these outer layers are virtually never found intact on a painted panel. Most panels used for paintings are cut from the dense heartwood of a tree, so scientists must add on a likely number of outer sapwood rings to arrive at a possible felling date. They must also consider how long the wood was allowed to season before it was sufficiently dry to be painted on – which, depending on local custom and individual practice, might vary from a minimum of two years to fifteen years or more. Despite the many limitations and variables, dendrochronology is useful for spotting incongruities between the felling date and the assumed date of a panel painting based on art historical evidence (case study 5). It can also identify panels that have been cut from the same tree, whether used in the same painting or different ones.

Most canvases and panels used for painting were prepared not by the artist but by specialised craftsmen, and occasionally bear labels or markings that identify the maker. For example, metal and

Right: 10. Anthony van
Dyck (1599–1641), *Rinaldo
conquered by Love for Armida*,
1634–5, oil on wood,
57 x 41.5 cm.

Below: 11. Detail of the back
of the wood panel support of
*Rinaldo conquered by Love for
Armida*, marked with the brand
of the city of Antwerp: two
hands and a stylised image of
a castle.

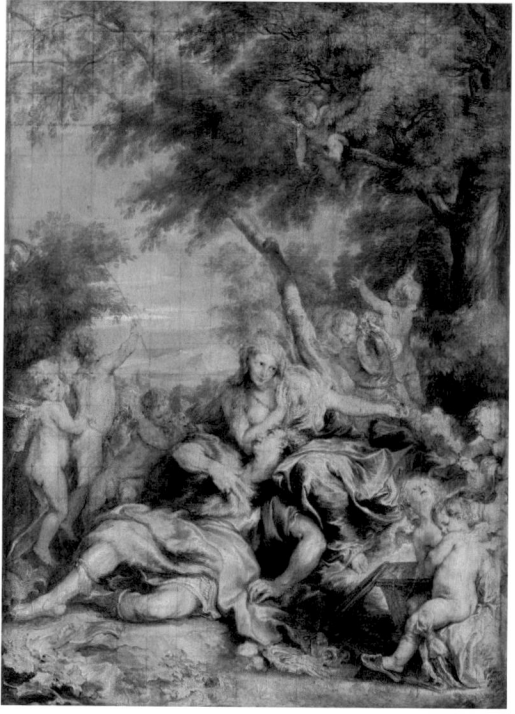

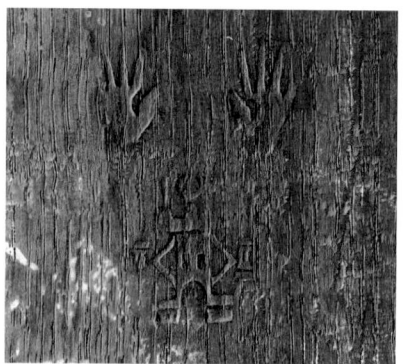

wood panels produced in Brussels and Antwerp were frequently
impressed or branded, both with that city's insignia and the mark
of the individual panel maker; this can help to verify a geographic
origin and approximate date for the painting support.

There are several examples of marked Antwerp panels in the
National Gallery, including Anthony van Dyck's *Rinaldo conquered
by Love for Armida*, which is painted on a panel bearing the brand
used by the city of Antwerp between 1619 and 1638 [10, 11].
It also features the incised initials of the panel maker Michiel
Vriendt (d. 1636/7).

Such labels and markings can confirm what is already known
about a painting based on art historical evidence (as in the case of
the Van Dyck) or they can furnish new information – sometimes
contrary to what is expected. For example, the supplier's mark on
the back of the National Gallery's small so-called *Self Portrait* of
Gustave Courbet presents something of a conundrum [12]. The
painting has long been regarded as the artist's own replica of his
large *Self Portrait*, painted in about 1845/6 and now in the Musée
d'Orsay, Paris. In 2008, as the painting was researched for the
Gallery's ongoing programme of re-cataloguing the collection, a
paper label on the back of the *Self Portrait* was found to bear the

12. After Gustave Courbet (1819–1877), *Self Portrait (L'Homme à la Ceinture de Cuir)*, after 1880, oil on board, 45 x 37.8 cm.

Below left and right: 13 and 14. The back of the millboard support of *Self Portrait* bears fragments of the Lefranc & Cie trade label, visible beneath a roughly painted sketch of a hand resting on a studio stool. The image on the right has been rotated 90 degrees anti-clockwise from the portrait painted on the front.

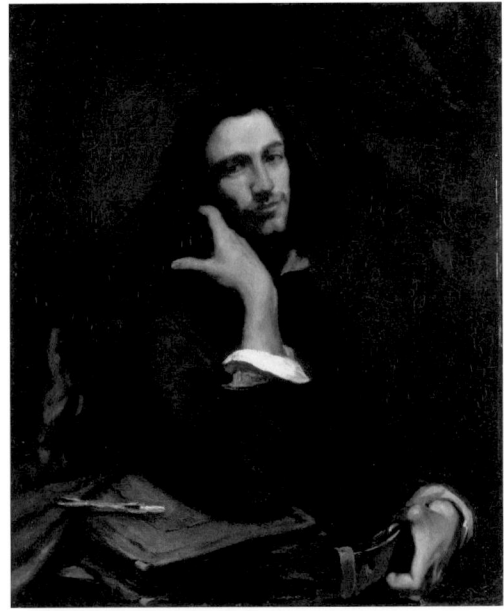

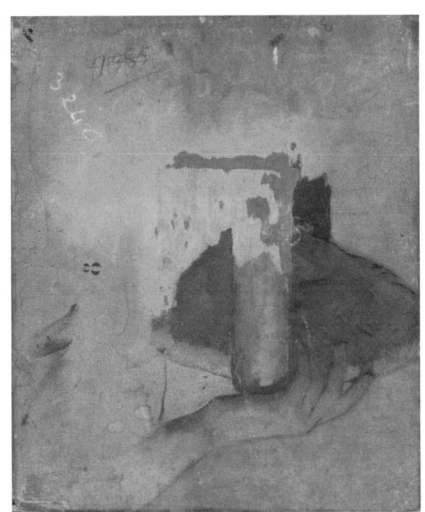

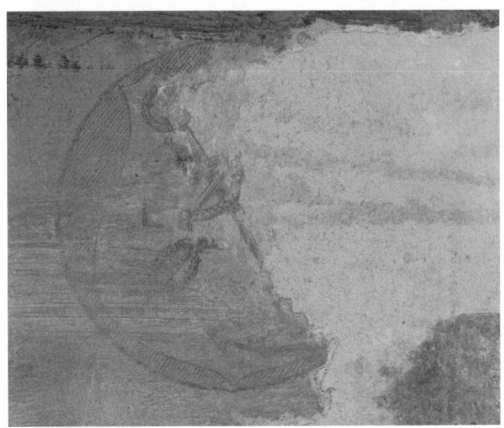

trademark used by the Parisian artists' supplier Lefranc & Cie. However, that particular trademark was registered only in 1880 – three years after Courbet's death [13, 14]. Further examination of the painting during a recent cleaning revealed that the panel was prepared with a white ground, an uncharacteristic choice for Courbet, who often favoured dark-toned grounds. The National Gallery's painting would thus seem to be a copy after the painting in Paris, made sometime between 1880 and 1912, when it is first recorded in a sale. Further research may yet uncover a name for the artist who painted it.

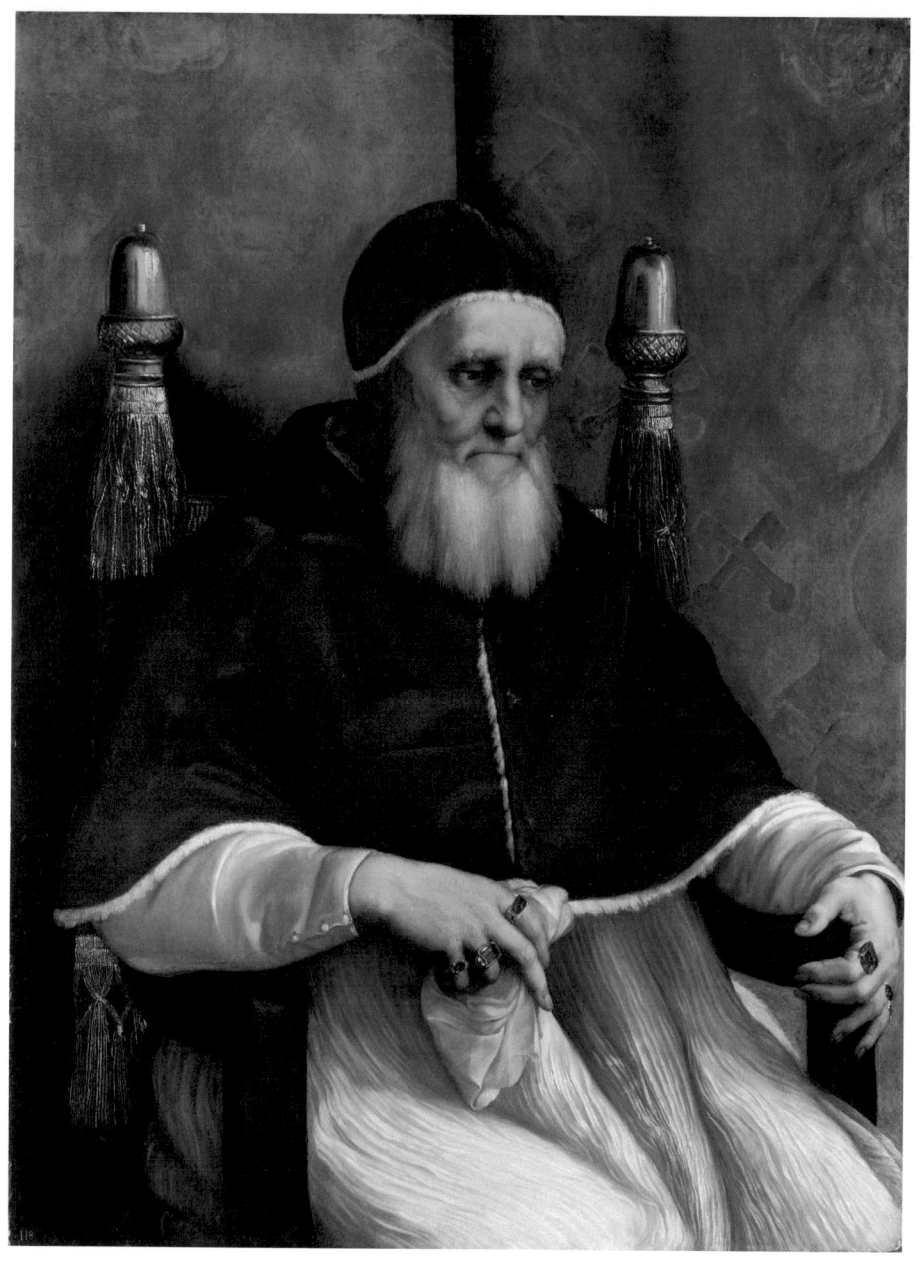

15. Raphael (1483–1520), *Portrait of Pope Julius II*, 1511, oil on poplar, 108.7 x 81 cm.

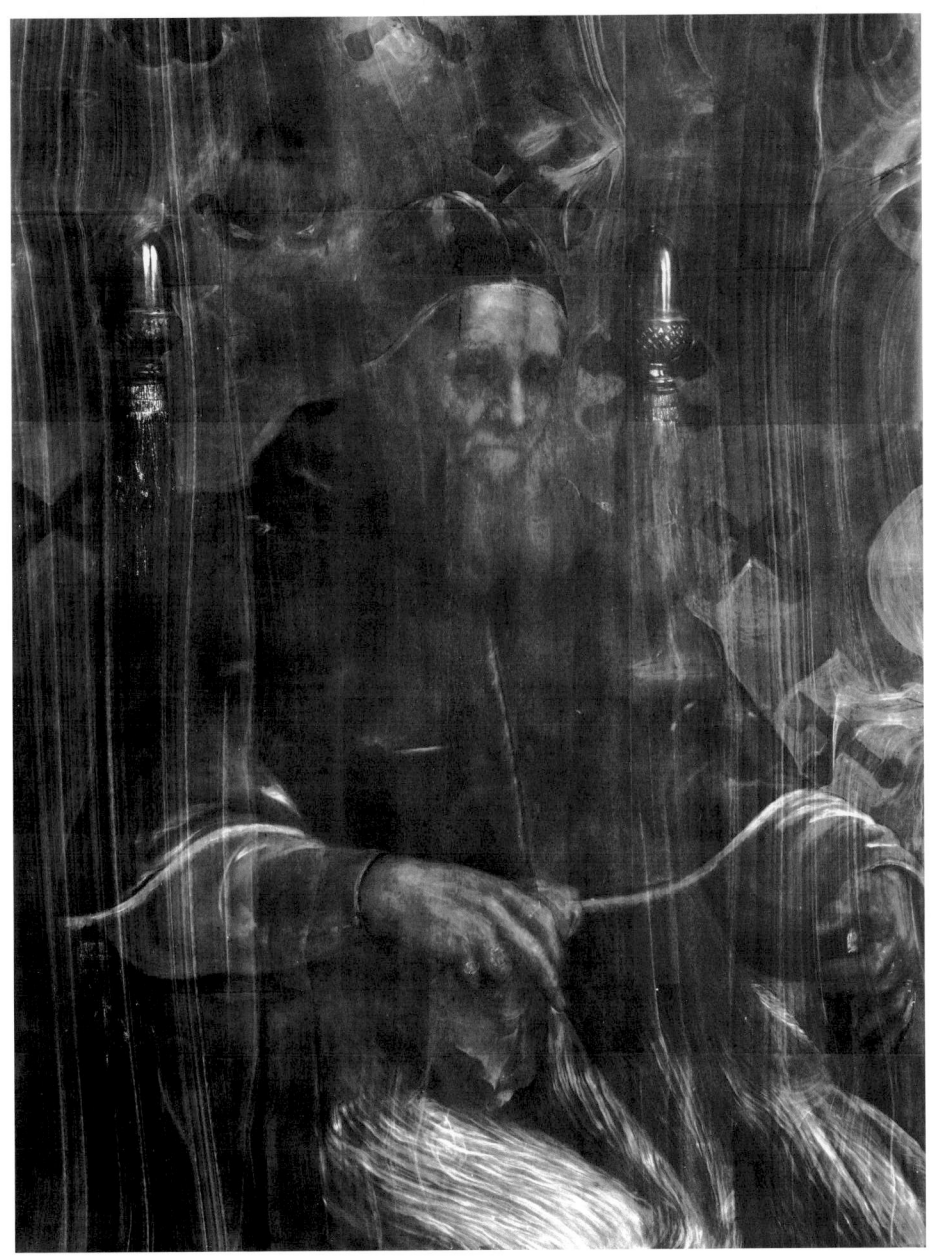

16. X-radiograph of *Portrait of Pope Julius II* showing the initial design for the background, which featured a repeating pattern of heraldic motifs. The vertical striations are caused by the grain of the wood panel.

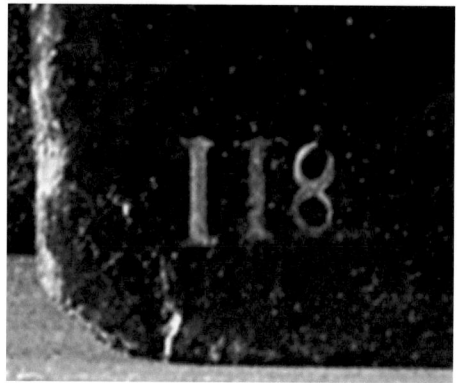 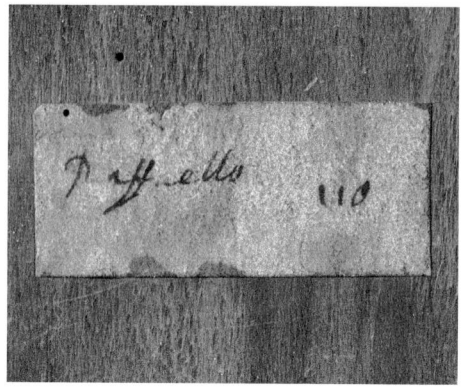

Above left: 17. Detail of the Borghese inventory number painted on *Portrait of Pope Julius II*, lower left corner.

Above right: 18. Inventory label on the reverse of *Portrait of Pope Julius II*.

Seals, labels and markings on paintings can also be a valuable source of information about past owners. For many years Raphael's *Portrait of Pope Julius II* [15] was thought to be an early copy of a version in the Uffizi, Florence, but in 1969 the dramatic discovery of two key pieces of evidence helped to confirm that the National Gallery's version was the original. X-radiographs, taken in response to a scholarly inquiry, showed numerous pentimenti, or changes made by the artist as he worked (p. 21), and during a subsequent cleaning a painted inventory number was revealed in the lower left corner of the picture [17]. Together with an old paper label on the back of the panel, this number matched a description of the portrait in an inventory of the Borghese collection in Rome, dating from 1693 [18]. From there, researchers could trace ownership of the painting back to its original placement in the Church of Santa Maria del Popolo in Rome. A letter written in 1513 confirmed that the pope himself had commissioned the portrait and given it to the church. The discovery of one small detail – a painted inventory number – was crucial to the rehabilitation of Raphael's magnificent painting.

Searching Beneath the Surface

While direct visual examination, with and without magnification, provides a wealth of information about a painting's creation and physical history, it cannot tell the whole story. Vital information lies hidden beneath the visible surface of the painting, buried by the very process of creation. Scientists must employ diverse methods of examination and analysis to probe beneath the surface and study every aspect of a painting's materials and methods of production. Imaging techniques, microscopic examination and

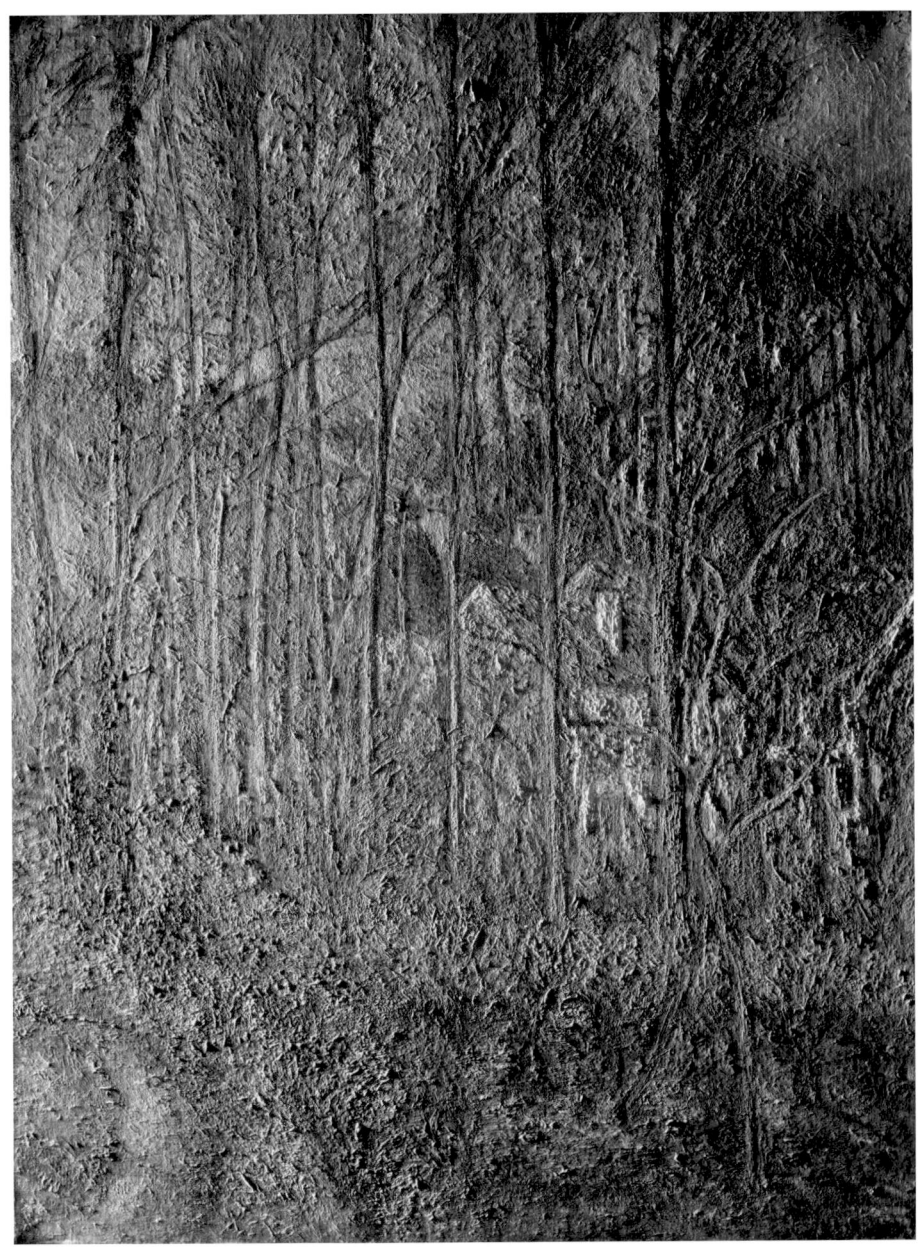

19. Camille Pissarro (1830–1903), *The Côte des Boeufs at L'Hermitage*, 1877, oil on canvas, 114.9 x 87.6 cm. Raking light accentuates the thickly textured surface of the painting.

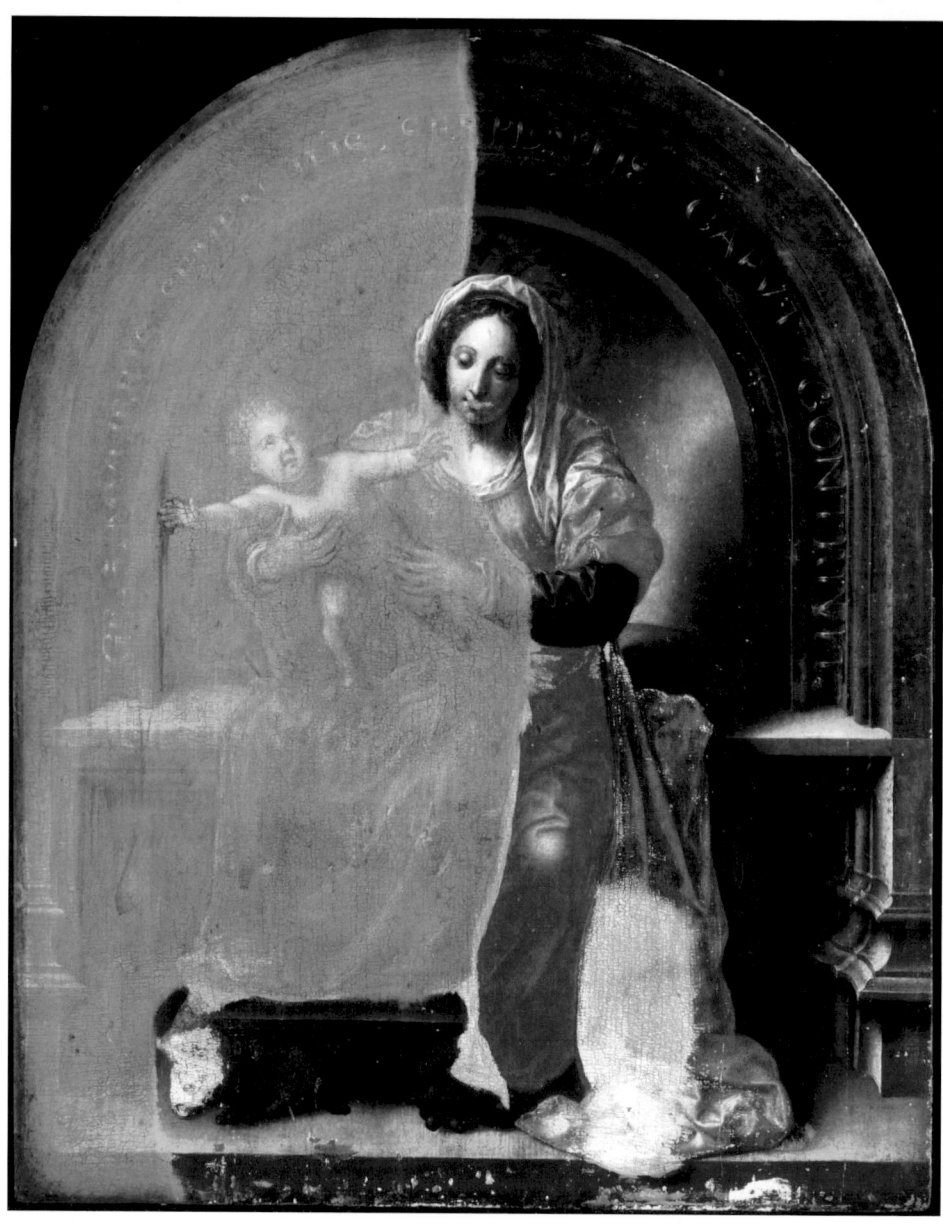

20. Jan Gossaert (active
1503; died 1532), *Virgin and
Child*, 1527, oil on oak, 30.5 x
23.5 cm. This photograph taken
during cleaning, with varnish
removed from the right half of
the painting. Under UV light,
the remnants of old varnish
on the left has a greenish
fluorescence. The bright pink
fluorescence on part of the
drapery on the lower right
indicates the presence of a
red lake pigment, probably
madder, applied in the
nineteenth century.

instrumental analyses can each provide a piece of the puzzle, and scientists typically use a combination of methods to gather the widest possible array of information.

The choice of techniques depends on the specific questions posed by the object, how appropriate this particular method of inquiry is to the object, and how likely it is that the examination will produce meaningful results. Real-life case studies, introduced here and explored in more detail later in this book, show how National Gallery experts employ a variety of scientific techniques to study the paintings in its collection.

One of the most straightforward techniques is to examine a picture with **raking light**. Directing light at an oblique angle to the painted surface exaggerates variations in texture and highlights distinctive aspects of the structure – such as seams or joins in the support, incisions or irregularities in the ground or changes in the texture of the paint layer that do not correspond to the visible design [19]. The presence of such anomalies often signals a need for further investigation. Raking light is particularly effective in revealing the qualities of **impasto** (paint applied thickly, showing the marks made by brush and palette knife) and raised paint texture of a surface.

Illumination of a painting with **ultraviolet light** can cause some painting materials to exhibit fluorescence, the colour of which may be characteristic for certain materials. It can thus help to identify areas of retouching, as well as certain pigments and different types of varnish. For example, a natural resin varnish which covers older paint fluoresces a light greenish colour. Areas of more recent retouching on top of the varnish do not fluoresce, however, and therefore typically appear dark under UV illumination [20].

X-radiography was first applied to the examination of paintings in around 1896, almost immediately after X-rays were discovered by Wilhelm Röntgen. The technique is relatively straightforward: one or more sheets of X-ray sensitive film are placed on the surface of the painting and X-rays are transmitted through the painting from underneath. Painting materials are more or less transparent to X-rays, according to their atomic constitution. More absorptive materials, such as lead-containing pigments or the iron tacks used to pin canvas to stretcher, block the penetration of X-rays and appear dark on the X-ray photograph when it is developed. (The image is usually printed as a photographic positive, rendering these dark areas light.) The resulting image is especially valuable in revealing **pentimenti** (alterations made by the artist in the course of painting) or an image that preceded the visible one, either an earlier stage of the painting or from a reused support. As an X-radiograph registers all layers of the painting at once, the superimposition of data can be confusing. However, it can be deciphered with experience, and in combination with other analytical techniques.

Several instances of how X-radiographs were key to understanding the development of a picture are discussed in the case studies below (case studies 9, 11, 13). Raphael's *Portrait of Pope Julius II* provides another dramatic example [figs 15, 16]. X-ray images made in 1969 revealed numerous pentimenti, including radical revisions to the background. Such compositional changes, together with other material evidence [p. 18], helped to confirm that the painting was indeed Raphael's original. The initial background – an alternating pattern of heraldic symbols (the papal tiara, crossed keys and Julius's family coat of arms) – was only partially finished before Raphael covered it with the simpler deep green backdrop that we see today. Guided by the X-ray image, scientists took minute samples to learn more about the underlying image. Microscopic analysis of the paint cross-sections indicated that the devices were painted in bright yellow against a blue background. Raphael probably realised that such a brightly patterned background would distract from his powerful and insightful depiction of the aged pope.

Infrared radiation (IR), the portion of the electromagnetic spectrum just beyond visible light, provides another way to see layers concealed below a painting's surface. Most commonly employed to study **underdrawings**, the artist's preliminary sketch made before the paint layers are applied, IR is also useful in revealing pentimenti and areas of damage and retouching. This is possible because pigments used in paint vary in opacity, depending on the wavelength of the light hitting them. Some pigments which are opaque in visible light become more transparent in the infrared region. This allows the infrared radiation to penetrate more deeply into the painting before being reflected back to the imaging device. Carbon black, a popular pigment for underdrawing, absorbs (rather than reflects) infrared radiation and thus appears dark in IR images, allowing underdrawn lines hidden beneath paint to be made visible (case studies 2, 5, 9, 12, 14, 15, 16). In addition to recording changes between the initial design and the final painting, the presence of a characteristic underdrawing can be instrumental in determining that a painting is the artist's original and not a copy.

Because infrared light cannot be seen by the human eye, scientists record images either by photographs using infrared-sensitive film or by **infrared reflectography (IRR)**, which uses a special camera sensitive further into the infrared region. Technological advances have improved the quality of infrared reflectography significantly since its development in the 1960s. Early IRR cameras were low resolution, so scientists had to record many small images and join them together to cover a whole painting. This often produced a rather patchy result. Recently, however, the National Gallery has been involved in developing a new IRR camera able to record images of much larger areas in one exposure. 'Reading' infrared images, like interpreting X-radiographs, is a complex process, and requires considerable experience to decipher multiple layers of superimposed data [21].

To discover more about a painting's layer structure and its constituent parts, it is generally necessary to take a minuscule sample for examination and analysis. Typically measuring less than 0.25 mm across, these samples are taken only from areas of pre-existing damage or hidden by the frame at the very edge of the painting. To study the layer structure of a painting, a cross-section is made by embedding the sample in a block of resin. The block is ground down to expose the sample edge-on, revealing successive layers of ground, paint and varnish. Scientists examine the cross-

21. Infrared reflectography (IRR) analysis in progress.

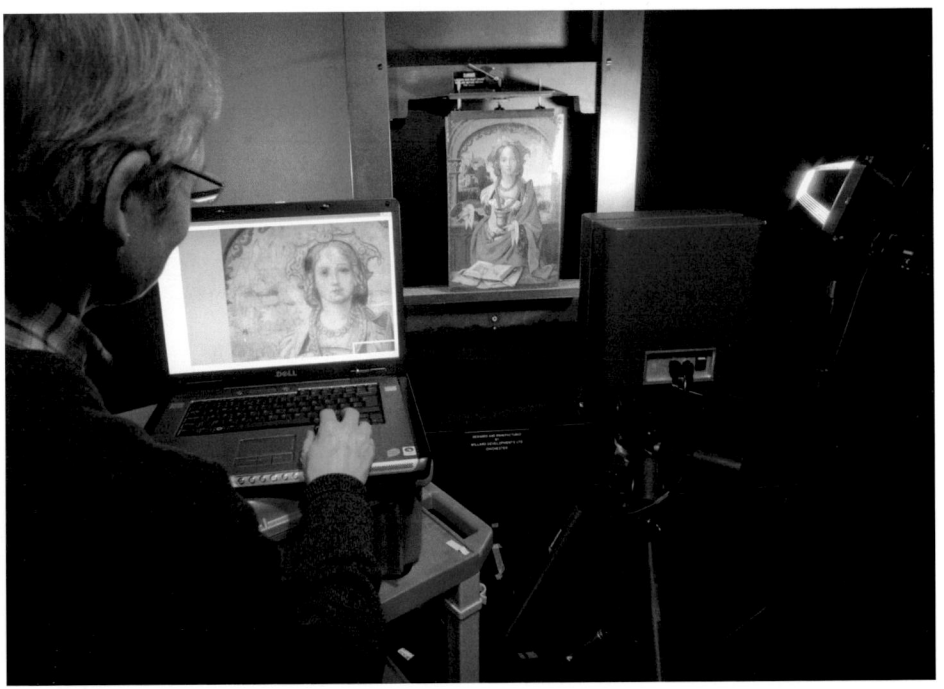

section at high magnification under the optical microscope to identify the different layers. Studying the strata can reveal how the composition evolved, and the chronology and extent of different painting campaigns (case study 10). It can also help to clarify changes seen in an X-radiograph, as demonstrated in the analysis of Raphael's *Portrait of Pope Julius II*.

Scientists also use cross-sections to study the optical properties – size, shape, colour, transparency, opacity and distribution – of pigment particles to identify individual pigments in a paint mixture. To assist in identifying organic materials (paint binding media, varnish, and so on), the cross-section is illuminated with ultraviolet light, a technique called **UV fluorescence microscopy**. As with surface examinations, under UV light certain materials may exhibit characteristic fluorescence. **Polarised light microscopy** involves a microscope equipped with a polarising light filter to investigate the characteristic crystalline structure of pigment particles in a sample [22]. To enable observation of a sample by transmitted polarised light, scientists prepare thin cross-sections by fixing the polished cross-section to a microscope slide and grinding and polishing the reverse to the required thickness (usually less than 20 **microns**). Dispersions of particles from particular paint layers may also be examined in this way.

A **scanning electron microscope (SEM)** is used for more detailed investigations. Scientists expose the sample to a narrow beam of high-energy electrons which interact with particles at or just below the surface of the sample. This interaction produces signals which can be collected using a variety of detectors. Images produced by secondary electron and back-scattered signals provide information about the sample's surface topography and chemical composition at magnifications up to 100,000×. The SEM also produces characteristic X-rays which can be analysed

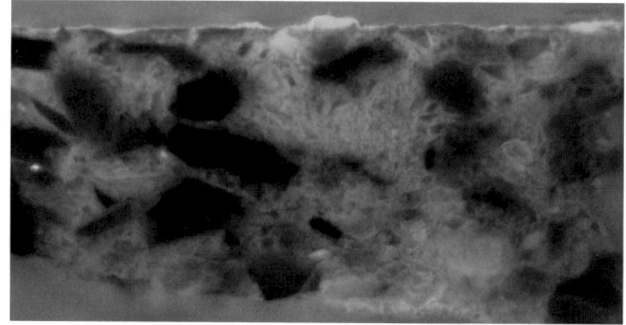

22. Cross-section of a sample taken from an area of dark blue drapery in *The Baptism of Christ* by Sassoferrato (case study 3). The paint layer consists of large particles of azurite in a now darkened binding medium. When viewed in UV light, as here, tiny particles of natural ultramarine, which fluoresces a pale yellow colour, become visible within the darkened medium.

Right: 23. A backscattered scanning electron image of a paint cross-section from *The Baptism of Christ* by Sassoferrato (case study 3). Tiny spherical particles of the synthetic pigment blue verditer are clearly visible. Blue verditer is combined with tiny particles of lead-tin yellow to produce the green paint of the foliage. The lead-tin yellow particles appear white in the image (due to their high atomic number) against a grey matrix of chalk (which has a low atomic number).

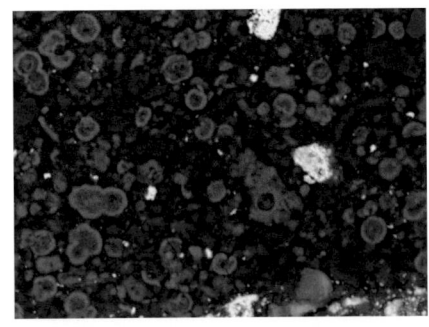

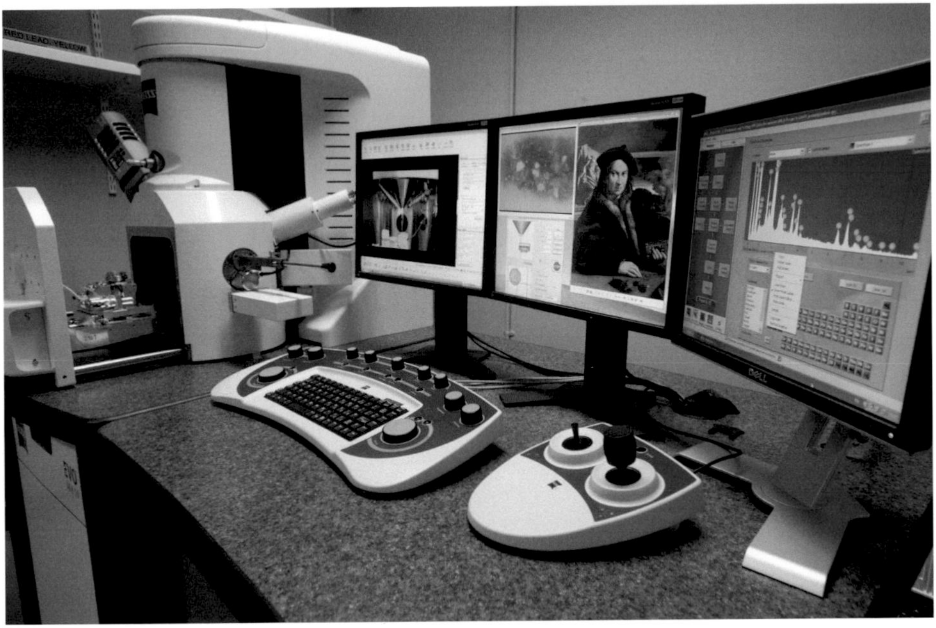

Above: 24. A cross-section from *Portrait of a Man* by Parmigianino undergoes EDX (energy dispersive X-ray) analysis at the National Gallery's Scientific Department. The scanning electron microscope (SEM) is a Zeiss (EVO MA1) variable pressure model, used with INCA EDX microanalysis.

using a technique known as **energy dispersive X-ray (EDX)** microanalysis [24]. With EDX, scientists can determine the elemental composition of a particular particle or layer within a cross-section. For the purposes of pigment identification, for example, the results can show whether the sample *contains* lead, copper, tin, arsenic, iron, cobalt, chromium and so on – but not what the actual component pigments *are*. Scientists must therefore interpret the data obtained by SEM–EDX analysis in conjunction with that gathered by optical microscopy in order to specify the pigments involved [23].

In particularly complex cases, elemental information and optical microscopy may not be sufficient to distinguish between closely related crystalline materials, including many pigments.

Scientists can also employ **X-ray diffraction (XRD)** analysis, a technique particularly suited to identifying fairly pure samples of crystalline pigments. The regular arrangement of atoms in a crystal scatters X-rays in a characteristic 'fingerprint' pattern, unique to that material. By identifying this pattern, XRD analysis allows unambiguous recognition of the material. XRD analysis played a key role in the technical analysis of the National Gallery's copy after Poussin's *The Plague at Ashdod*. The specific identification in the painting of lead-tin-antimony yellow pigment, the use of which seems to have been characteristic of seventeenth-century Rome, helped to establish that this was the well-documented copy produced by Poussin's contemporary, Angelo Caroselli (case study 4).

XRD can provide precise identification of crystalline materials in a compound, but an alternative method of analysis available to scientists in these difficult cases is **Raman microscopy**. This technique employs a low-powered laser beam to identify the molecular structure of inorganic and organic pigments with a high degree of sensitivity and specificity. Under the laser beam, each substance in the sample scatters a specific combination of wavelengths (known as its Raman spectrum) that can be regarded as its characteristic fingerprint. The recorded peaks of the individual material's Raman spectrum are compared against a spectral database. Because of its high spatial resolution (less than 1 micron), Raman microscopy is particularly useful for identifying the components of pigment mixtures. Using this technique, scientists were able to confirm the presence of lead-tin-antimony yellow in a copy after Perugino's *The Baptism of Christ*, proving that the copy was produced in the seventeenth and not the nineteenth century (case study 3).

To identify the paint binding medium, scientists routinely use two processes. The first, **FTIR (Fourier transform infrared) spectroscopy**, works on the principle that different materials absorb infrared radiation at different wavelengths [25]. A beam of infrared radiation is directed through the paint sample, and the specific wavelengths absorbed by each material are recorded as peaks on a spectrum. The location and relative intensity of the series of peaks gives a molecular fingerprint that can identify the material with reasonable certainty. Complex mixtures, such as those found in paint samples, can be difficult to interpret, but FTIR microscopy can be used to screen for the presence of certain types of organic binding materials (such as egg, oil or resin) or inorganic pigments (such as lead white, malachite,

25. An FTIR microscope in use at the Scientific Department of the National Gallery

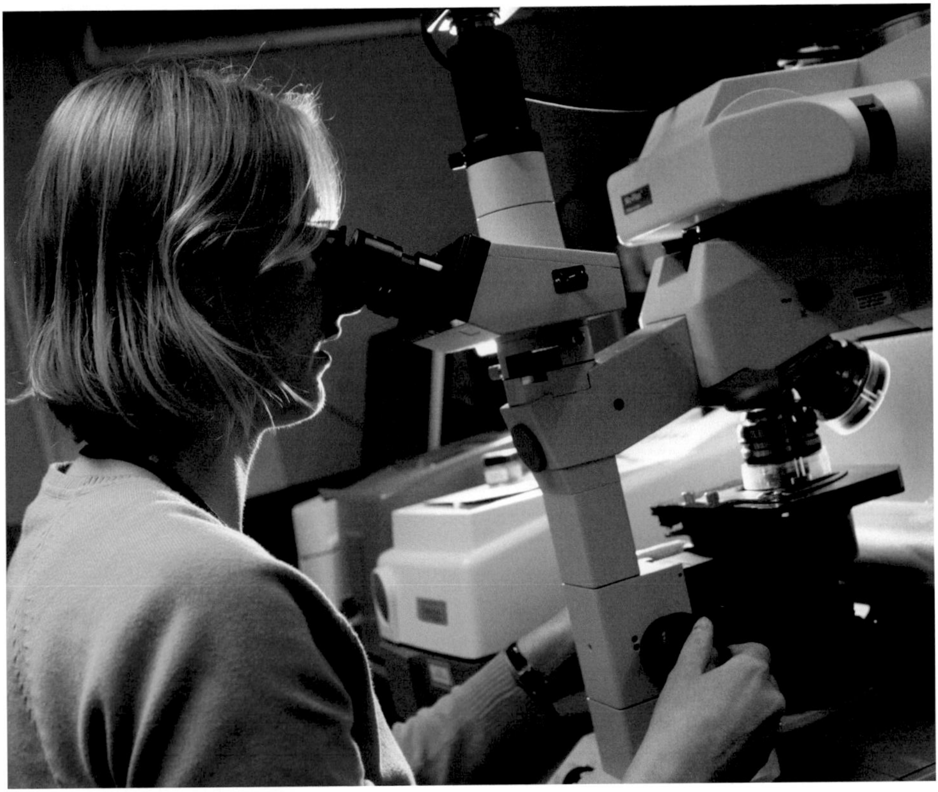

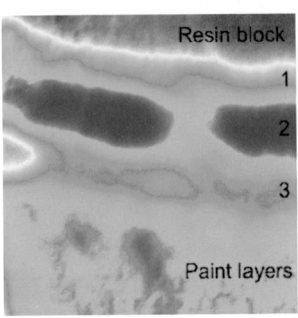

26. A 'chemical map' of a cross-section from the *Portrait Group* (case study 1) obtained using ATR-FTIR microscopy, a technique closely related to the FTIR method described in the text. The production of a painting which superficially mimicked that of a fifteenth-century Italian work required the use of materials and techniques not usually present in an authentic painting of the period. In this example, three incongruous layers (labelled 1, 2 and 3) were observed above the paint.

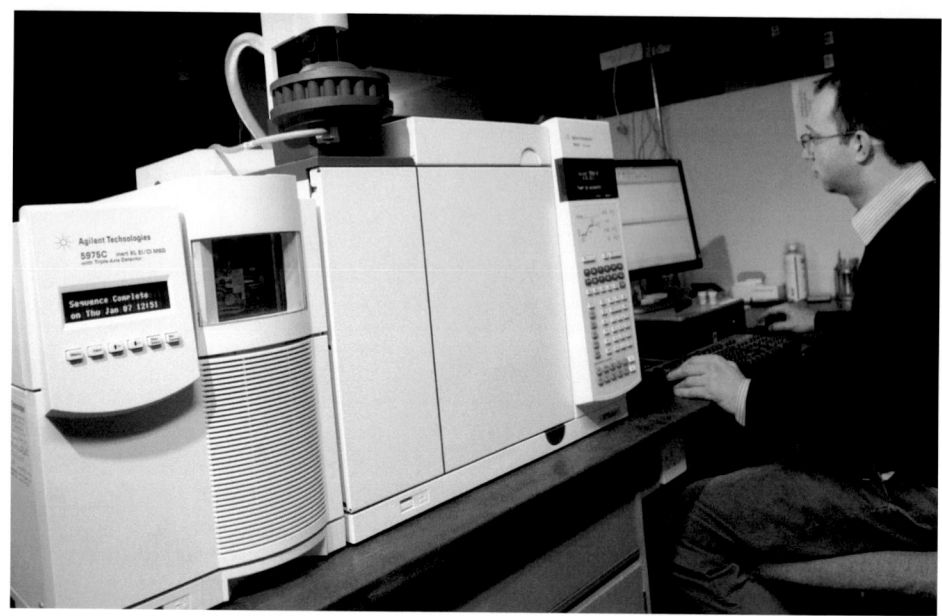

27. The gas chromatography-mass spectrometry (GC-MS) instrument currently used in the Scientific Department for the analysis of organic materials from paint samples.

ochre, etc). For example, when scientists examined the mysterious 'Italian' *Portrait Group* with FTIR, they were able to identify various unusual materials – including shellac or nitrocellulose – that the unknown forger used to create a convincingly 'aged' Renaissance painting (p. 36, case study 1). FTIR is also used to study how particular materials age. Over time, reactions between pigment and binder can form new chemical products. By observing certain characteristic peaks in the infrared spectrum, scientists can confirm the presence of these products.

More precise characterisation of organic materials in complex paint samples involves separating all the components by a technique known as **chromatography**. For gas chromatography, scientists usually extract the paint-binding medium from the sample with solvents and inject the solution into a stream of inert carrier gas. This is propelled through a heated capillary column, causing the molecular components of the sample to separate according to their chemical and physical properties. The molecules emerge from the gas chromatograph at different times, allowing the attached **mass spectrometer** to provide information on the molecular structure of each separated component. The results obtained from this **GC-MS analysis** enable similar materials to be distinguished from one another, allowing scientists to identify (for instance) the particular type of

28. GC-MS analysis of a paint fragment containing an original varnish layer from Dosso Dossi, *A Man embracing a Woman* (pp. 70–2) confirmed the presence of the molecule sandaracopimarate, shown here with its mass spectrum, indicating the use of sandarac resin.

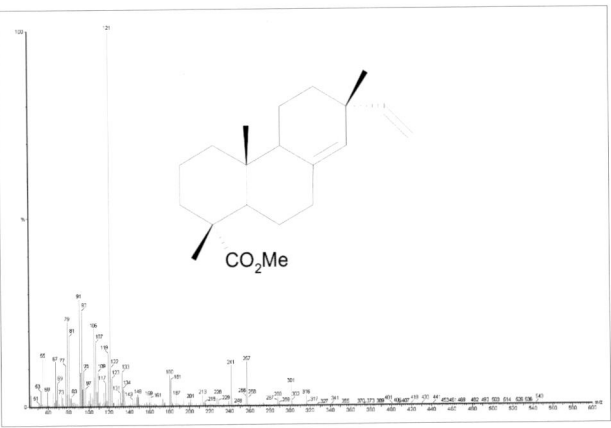

oil or resin [27]. In the case of Dosso Dossi's *A Man embracing a Woman*, GC-MS analysis resulted in the identification of a rare surviving example of an original sixteenth-century varnish, sandwiched between the paint layers (case study 11). Like FTIR, GC-MS analysis can also be used to study the products of degrading or degraded materials. The related technique of **High Performance Liquid Chromatography (HPLC)** uses a liquid to carry the sample through a column of porous material. The individual molecular components are separated as they gradually move through the column. HPLC is most often used to identify organic dyes (case study 2).

The development of non-invasive methods of studying works of art – with the goal of performing analyses without the need for samples – has aroused particular interest in recent years. Many of these techniques are adaptations of older analytical technologies, based on vibrational spectroscopy (including infrared and Raman) or fluorescence spectroscopy. Others are extensions of techniques such as non-contact **X-ray fluorescence analysis (XRF)**, capable of elemental analysis of surfaces and layers just beneath the surface. Physicists and materials scientists are also exploring ways to apply examination methods developed in other spheres, particularly medical technology and engineering, to the analysis of paintings and other works of art. For example, X-ray tomographic techniques and optical coherence tomography (OCT) both show promise in imaging features beneath the surfaces of objects, in a similar way to a medical CT scan. A current and growing trend in scientific analysis takes advantage of the facilities of high-energy physics research, such as particle accelerators, harnessing synchrotron radiation sources (at various wavelengths and energies) for the analysis of works of art and material taken from them. However, it is unlikely that these techniques could ever become truly routine in museums or at historic sites.

Much progress has been made, and significant developments in non-invasive analytical techniques will undoubtedly take place in the decades to come. However, the crucial problem of revealing and interpreting the physical and chemical make-up of complex, multilayered objects (a category which includes most easel paintings) has so far remained rather intractable to these newer techniques. For scientists, restorers, curators and art historians, examination and analysis of paint cross-sections is still the best way to extract the most detailed and reliable information on a painting's material constitution, although newer methods are beginning to provide supplementary results. Rapid changes are also taking place in the means of analysing paint microsamples in cross-section. Scientists have developed chemical imaging methods to provide detailed analytical information in the form of 'chemical maps' [26]; these work at a level of microscopic resolution in a paint layer structure.

This brief overview has concentrated on techniques routinely used by scientists at the National Gallery. It has not tried to cover every tool available to researchers, not least because methods of analysis and approaches to scientific examination are constantly evolving. The speed of technological advance continues to increase, and scientists mine the most promising innovations for their potential to improve or expand our understanding of paintings and other works of art. As new equipment and processes are developed, and new or more refined applications appear, technical research will undoubtedly yield many more exciting discoveries about the paintings housed in museums and galleries.

Weighing the Evidence

Perhaps the single most important stage of any scientific examination – regardless of how simple or how complex – is the careful and informed interpretation of results. Scientists, curators and restorers must always consider the accumulated data in the context of that particular painting. The presence of a specific material might be entirely customary and appropriate for one painting, but if discovered in another could trigger serious concerns about that picture's authenticity or date. The study

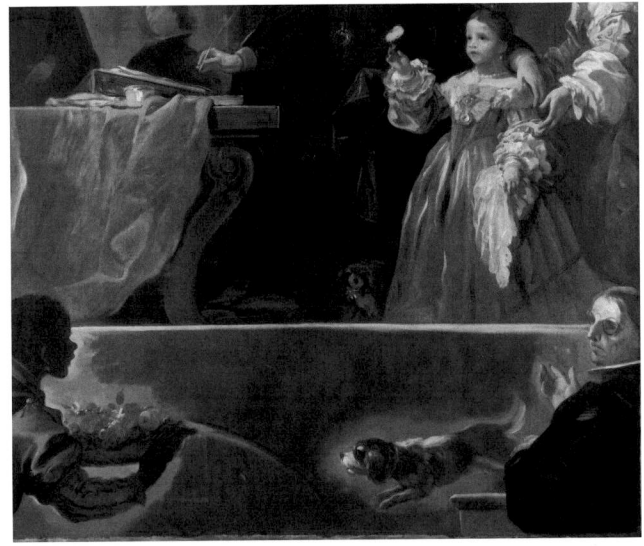

29. Detail of Luca Giordano (1634–1705), *A Homage to Velázquez*, about 1692–1700, oil on canvas, 205.2 x 182.2 cm. This detail from an unfinished painting shows how Giordano quickly sketched the basic forms of the figures over a warm brown ground.

of historical painting techniques, materials and studio practice relies upon gathering a large body of comparative material. Collecting and analysing such information – both from original documentary sources and the results of extensive research on materials – has long been a focus of the National Gallery's work.

In any given era, artists have a common range of pigments and media at their disposal. However, it is in the *method* of using these materials (pigment mixtures, variations in binding media, layer structure or ways of applying paint) that experts can observe differences between workshops, periods within the era or local practice. To take just one example, researchers can look for certain features in the preparatory ground layer to help clarify when and where a painting was produced. In Italy *gesso* (Italian for gypsum, calcium sulphate) was typically used for the ground layer, but calcium carbonate (natural chalk) was used in northern Europe; both were bound in a medium of animal skin glue. Thus, although the National Gallery's *River Landscape*, based on a composition by the Flemish artist Pieter Bruegel the Elder, has traditionally been catalogued as a sixteenth-century Netherlandish painting, the fact that it is painted on a poplar panel prepared with a gesso ground strongly suggests that it was painted in Italy.

A coloured ground in a painting can also help to determine its approximate date, as we know strongly coloured grounds, particularly oil-based ones, became widespread from the late sixteenth and through the seventeenth centuries [29]. This particular knowledge was significant in the re-evaluation of a copy after a work by the Renaissance artist Pietro Perugino, which we now know to have been painted in the seventeenth and not the nineteenth century (case study 3).

A continuing area of research at the National Gallery concerns the history of use of artists' materials, both natural and synthetic. Subject to availability, cost, tradition and personal choice, painters have explored the creative potential of various earth and mineral pigments – as well as animal and vegetable dyes and a variety of paint binding media. From the early eighteenth century painters' palettes were greatly expanded with the introduction of modern synthetic pigments, a process which accelerated enormously in the nineteenth century. When scientists identify pigments with a well-documented date of introduction in an area of original paint, they can determine the earliest date that work could have been made. They can also establish and date which parts were later additions to the painting (case studies 1, 3, 12, 13, 14). One particularly graphic example of a later addition to a painting is the *Portrait of Alexander Mornauer* (case study 12). For many years the portrait sported a striking blue background which, when analysed, was found to contain Prussian blue, a pigment that only came into use over two centuries after the original painting was made. The presence of the same pigment on the painted ledge in Botticelli's *Saint Francis of Assisi with Angels* alerted scientists and researchers to the fact that this area – and the inscription and date it contained – was a later (and, as it turned out, erroneous) addition (case study 14).

Other materials disappeared from painters' palettes as new pigments came into use, allowing for a 'latest possible' dating in works containing that pigment. The use of lead-tin-antimony yellow pigment, for example, seems to have had its origins in paintings produced in Italy during the seventeenth century, so confirming the presence of this pigment in two of the paintings studied here enabled scientists to determine that they were not later works (case studies 3 and 4).

Although pigment analysis and identification cannot date a painting precisely, discovering anachronisms in its materials can be a straightforward way to detect later copies and forgeries. There are two clear-cut examples of this in the Gallery's collection. The Italian *Portrait Group*, which was believed to be a fifteenth-century work, was found to contain nineteenth-century synthetic pigments such as cadmium yellow and cobalt blue, as well as other modern materials used to create a deceptive appearance of age (case study 1). And when scientists recently examined *The Virgin and Child with an Angel*, for many years considered an original

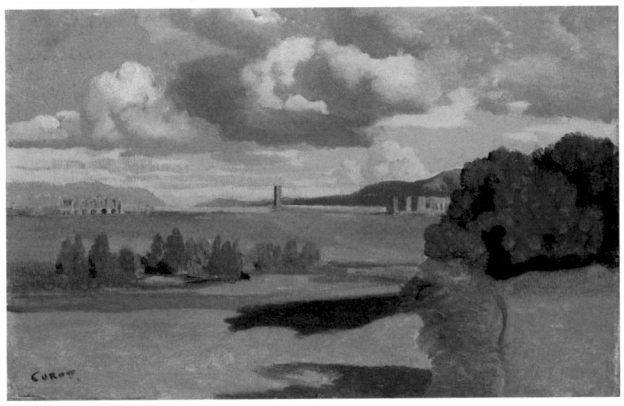

30. Jean-Baptiste-Camille Corot (1796–1875), *The Roman Campagna, with the Claudian Aqueduct*, probably 1826, oil on paper, laid on canvas, 22.8 x 34 cm.

work by Francesco Francia dated 1490, they found chrome yellow, another nineteenth-century synthetic pigment, in the original paint layer (case study 2).

The history of the materials and techniques of painting is a useful tool for geographically locating or dating paintings, but there can be pitfalls in basing assumptions on a single piece of information. Occasional and notable exceptions to accepted chronologies emphasise the dangers. For example, Jean-Baptiste-Camille Corot painted the small but dramatic sketch of *The Roman Campagna, with the Claudian Aqueduct* a few months after he arrived in Rome in late 1825 [30]. For the most part, the pigments he used are conventional for the period – with the exception of the synthetic green pigment viridian, found throughout the painting, but most prominently in the mid-green strip extending from the left-hand side. Viridian (transparent hydrated chromium oxide) was first manufactured by the artist-chemist Antoine-Claude Pannetier, and researchers believed it to have been available to artists only from the late 1830s. But this date seems to contradict the date of about 1826 given to Corot's painting on stylistic grounds. Only recently has it been realised that Pannetier must have made his viridian pigment available through a single artists' supplier in Paris as early as the 1820s. Corot is known to have been a customer of this firm even before he left for Italy in 1825, and he was probably one of the first to experiment with the new green pigment before it became widely available. Corot's clear and rapid development as a painter means that his early paintings can frequently be dated with a high degree of specificity. In this instance, the strong stylistic and historical evidence for dating *The Roman Campagna* to 1826 encouraged researchers to take a closer look at contemporary documents to make sense of the puzzling scientific data.

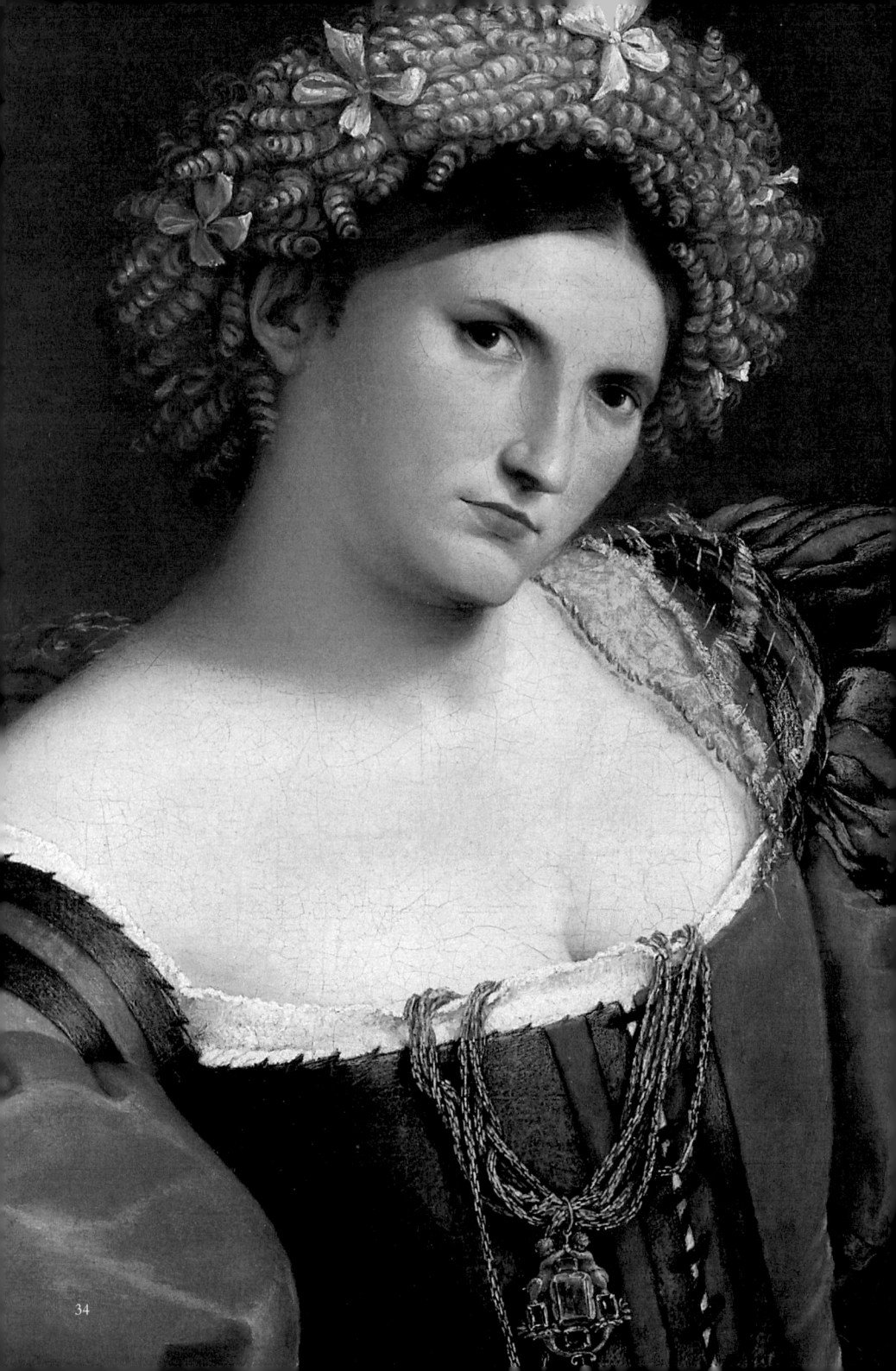

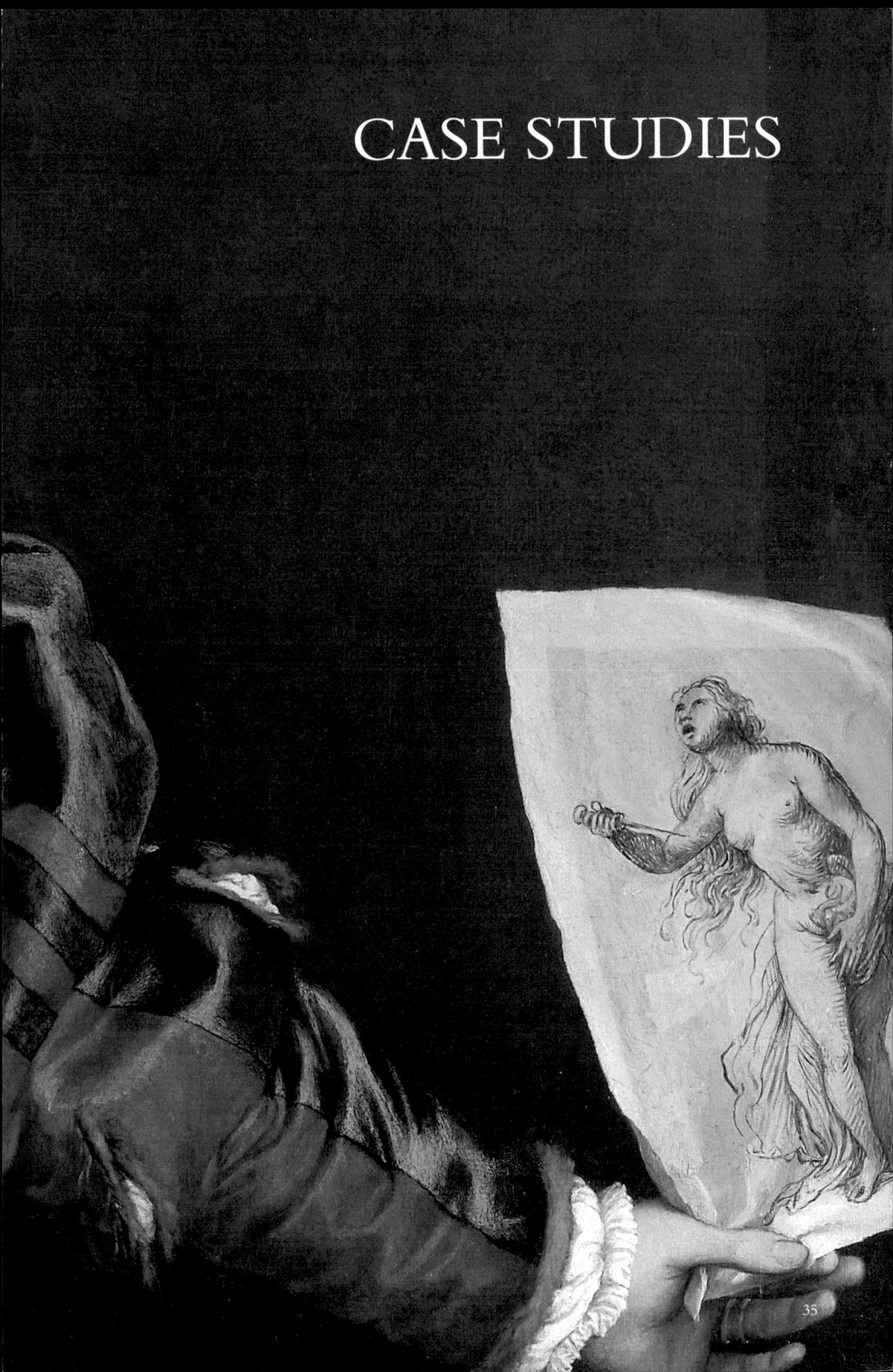

CASE STUDIES

CASE STUDY 1:
A GENUINE FAKE

Italian, *Portrait Group*, early twentieth century

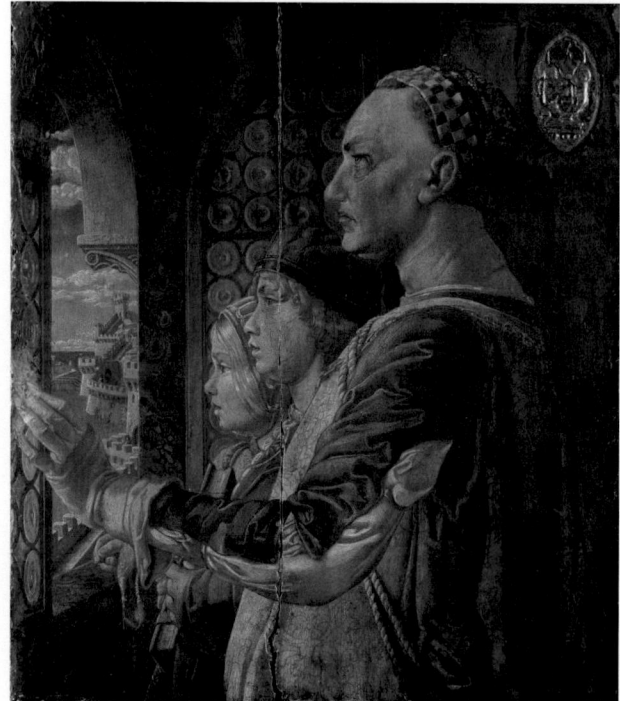

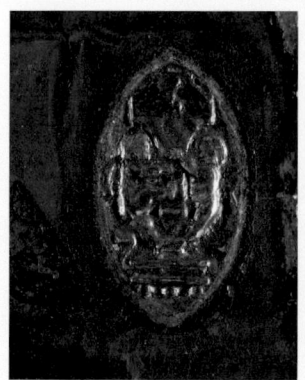

Left: 31. Italian, *Portrait Group*, early twentieth century, oil and tempera on wood, 40.6 x 36.5 cm.

Above: 32. Detail of the *Portrait Group* showing the armorial badge stamped in gesso at upper right.

This portrait of a man and two children was acquired by the National Gallery in 1923 as an Italian painting of the late fifteenth century, possibly by an accomplished but unknown artist in the circle of Melozzo da Forli. Until 1951 the painting was catalogued as a portrait of members of the Montefeltro family of Urbino, an identification based on the armorial badge stamped into the gesso at upper right [32, 34]. Pinpointing the identities of the individuals proved problematic, however, as no family members of the appropriate age and gender could be found.

From the start, the painting's unique physical properties puzzled researchers. Notes made at the time of acquisition describe the painted surface as 'very hard and possibly glazed with oil, covered with an old brown & exceedingly tough varnish: paint damaged in places by old worm holes & abrasions'. The peculiarly impervious nature of the paint in particular attracted attention, 'painted in tempera of an almost flinty substance, covered with a curiously hard brown varnish'. In April 1924 the restorer A.H. Buttery examined the painting thoroughly, largely to quell doubts about its authenticity

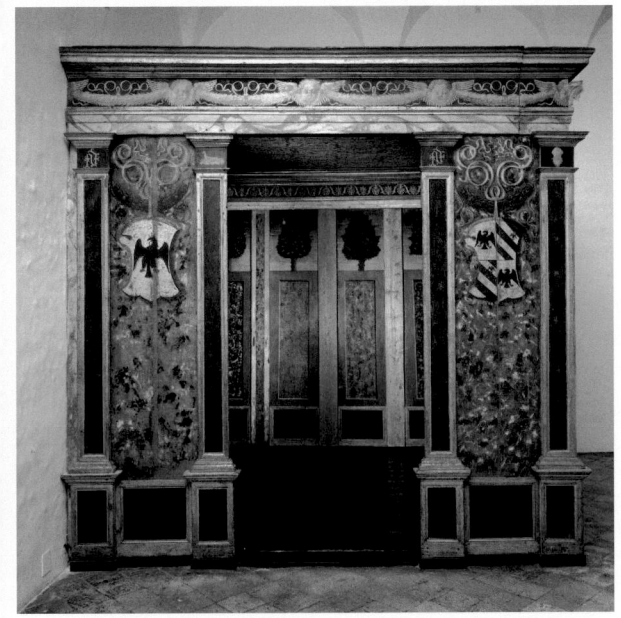

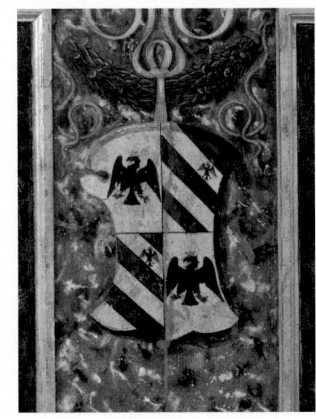

Left, and detail above:
33, 34. An alcove in
the Ducal Palace, Urbino,
showing the coat of arms of
Federico da Montefeltro.

voiced by a small but influential group of critics and art historians. Buttery's first impression was that it was an authentic painting of the fifteenth century: 'He then proceeded to test this view by heat and by applying pure solvent to various portions of the picture… He failed to move more than the varnish… His verdict was that the picture is beyond doubt a XVth century painting, and he congratulated the Trustees on having bought it at considerably below his own estimate of its value.' Armed with these results, the National Gallery issued a statement announcing that the painting's antiquity 'was again conclusively demonstrated'.

Twelve years later, however, C.J. Holmes (director of the National Gallery at the time of the acquisition) admitted that the *Portrait Group* 'remains a problem', and by 1951 the rueful assessment of the Earlier Italian Schools catalogue was that 'this picture appears to be modern'. Suspicions about the modern origins of the painting gathered strength in 1960, when Stella Mary Newton, a well-known costume historian, was able to demonstrate that the

garments worn by the figures were 'impossible in construction and inconsistent in date'. Male and female garments were randomly mixed, and the man's odd chequered cap was shown to be directly inspired by a distinctive women's fashion of about 1913.

Even well after it was realised that the *Portrait Group* was a forgery, the more curious technical aspects of the painting remained largely unexplored. In 1996–7, however, extensive scientific examination began to piece together details of how the picture was crafted. It was painted on a thin wood panel, subsequently stuck on to a thicker panel of old wood and artifically cracked vertically down the middle to heighten the impression of great age. The traditional gesso ground and egg tempera medium were used, the latter confirmed by GC-MS analysis and FTIR microscopy (pp. 26–7). However, SEM-EDX analysis identified a number of modern pigments in the samples: cobalt blue, cadmium yellow, viridian and chrome yellow. None of these were available before the nineteenth century. The paint layer

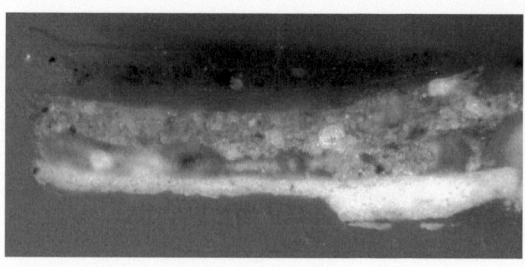

35. Cross-section of the *Portrait Group*. A layer of shellac was applied over a layer of paint containing the nineteenth-century pigment cobalt blue. Just above is a thin, darker brown layer which may be animal glue, deliberately tinted to further 'age' the painting.

is covered with a layer of shellac, a yellowish resin secretion from the lac insect, mixed with pine colophony, a translucent amber substance distilled from turpentine oleoresin [35]. This was probably a cheap, commercially prepared varnish. Covering the shellac is a proteinaceous layer which has been deliberately tinted, presumably to give the appearance of age, before the final varnish layer was applied. These upper layers produced the curiously 'flinty' character and brownish tonality of the deceptively aged surface. In addition, the shellac was well 'keyed' into the paint layer, and it is likely that as it dried it contracted, producing a pronounced craquelure in the paint below. Superficially at least, this simulated the surface craquelure typical for paintings of the fifteenth century.

Although scientific investigation has yielded considerable information about the methods used to manufacture the painting, it has brought us little closer to discovering who might have devised such a complex and sophisticated forgery. A note in the National Gallery's files describes the reaction of Alexander Crane, pupil of the Italian restorer and master forger Icilio Federico Joni, upon seeing a photograph of the picture in 1929: he was 'inclined to its being by Joni', finding the figures very characteristic, 'tho' the crackle [craquelure] is not as good as Joni usually has'. Crane later confronted Joni himself with a photograph of the painting: 'Finally … he said "*mi pare che non è antico*" ["this does not look old to me"] – which is to me as good as an acknowledgement of it being his manufacture.' Despite Crane's assertion, there is no positive

evidence of Joni having painted the *Portrait Group*, and indeed it bears little resemblance to his usual output of forgeries simulating Sienese paintings of the fourteenth and early fifteenth centuries. It is conceivable that Joni may have 'claimed' authorship of the *Portrait Group* in order to obscure his actual production, or Crane may simply have misinterpreted his mentor's response. In his memoirs, Joni frequently complained of having fakes attributed to him that he had not painted. Recently it has been suggested that one of Joni's contemporaries, Umberto Giunti, may have painted the work.

In hindsight, it seems surprising that this painting could ever have been mistaken for an authentic Italian portrait of the late fifteenth century, even without the evidence revealed by modern scientific analysis. The heightened linearity, especially that of the faces in strict profile, with their ribbon-like hair, seems a coarse exaggeration of the delicate clarity of fifteenth-century profile portraits. The faces themselves seem just a little too modern, the costumes and landscape view a little out of place. However, an early twentieth-century viewer could easily have discounted features made familiar by the taste of his own age: details that now appear inappropriately modern would for those viewers simply have proven the 'ageless' appeal of Renaissance painting. He or she might well have been captivated by a painting that seemed to offer – *too* conveniently, as it turned out – everything the connoisseur of Renaissance painting could desire.

CASE STUDY 2:
A CLEVER AND CONVINCING COPY

After Francesco Francia,
The Virgin and Child with an Angel, probably
second half of the nineteenth century

The Virgin and Child with an Angel entered the
National Gallery's collection in 1924 as a work
by Francesco Francia. It was part of a generous
bequest by Ludwig Mond (1839–1909), a
wealthy businessman who had acquired the
picture in 1893 from the Roman dealer
Wilhelm Haass; its earlier history is not known.
Although not the most prominent painting in
Mond's collection (which included masterpieces
by Botticelli, Raphael, Titian and others), it was
of particular interest as Francia's earliest known
dated painting (faintly signed and dated 1490)
and for representing, in the chalice held by the
angel, the only known example of the type of
object Francia may have produced during his
presumed earlier career as a goldsmith.

In 1954 an apparently identical version of the
composition surfaced in a London auction [37].
Purchased by the London art dealer Leonard
Koetser, this new discovery was compared
against the National Gallery's painting and was
determined to be the original. Indeed, though
he discreetly kept his opinion to himself at the
time, National Gallery director Philip Hendy
'had no doubt as soon as I saw the two versions
side by side that Mr Koetser's was the original'.
Buoyed by a flood of sensationalist journalism,
the popular David versus Goliath story was
nonetheless grounded in a close scientific
investigation of the National Gallery's painting.

The 1955 examination found the painting's
wood panel, ground and paint layers to be
reasonably consistent with fifteenth-century
practice, although it was noted that the gesso
ground was 'whiter and finer' than normally
seen in Italian paintings of the period. The
pinkish-brown *imprimitura* covering the ground
would be most unusual in a painting of 1490,
but a similar one had been observed in a
slightly later painting by Francia in the National
Gallery's collection, the *Virgin and Child with
Two Saints* of about 1500–10. Microscopic
examination of pigments, both on the surface
and in cross-section, interpreted the green
lining of the Virgin's robe as containing a green
'copper resinate' pigment mixed with black and
brown to darken the colour, a technique then
unrecorded in Italian pictures of the period.

A comparison of the X-ray images taken
of both paintings was more decisive. It showed
the National Gallery's work to be rather thinly
painted, in contrast to the more traditional
layered build-up of paint evident in the
other version. Microscopic examination of
the former's craquelure aroused even greater
suspicion: the 'cracks' were actually painted on
the surface of the painting itself to mimic the
appearance of a naturally aged paint surface. In
1955 the National Gallery acknowledged that
its painting was probably a nineteenth-century
fake and that the rediscovered painting, now in
the collection of the Carnegie Museum of Art,
Pittsburgh, was Francia's original.

In the late 1990s, a scholarly inquiry
prompted a renewed investigation of the
painting which led to a rather different –
but still inconclusive – interpretation of the
technical evidence. Once again, the unusually
bright white gesso ground and the pink
imprimitura were signalled as 'noteworthy but
not suspicious'. The painted 'cracks' were seen
as a restorer's attempt to harmonise modern
retouchings with the condition of the painting
as a whole, while the unusual mix of pigments
in the green lining of the Virgin's robe was
similarly explained as a later restoration. It was
suggested that the National Gallery's painting

Below left: 36. After Francesco Francia (about 1450–1517/18), *The Virgin and Child with an Angel*, probably second half of the nineteenth century, oil on wood, 58.5 x 44.5 cm.

Below right: 37. Francesco Francia (about 1450–1517/18), *The Virgin and Child with an Angel*, about 1490, oil on wood, 58 x 44 cm. Carnegie Museum of Art, Pittsburgh; Museum Purchase, 1973 (73.9). Technical analysis has confirmed that this painting, rediscovered in 1954, is Francia's original.

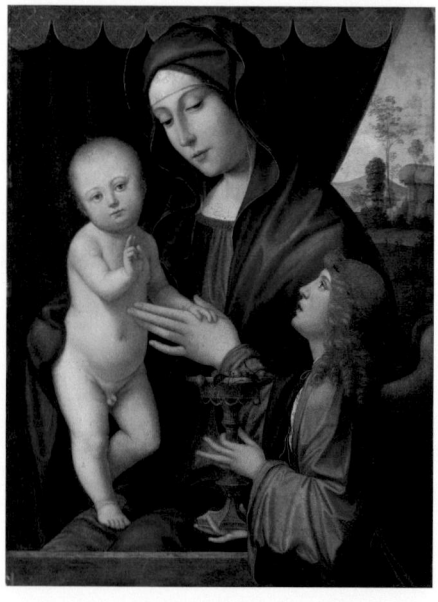

might well be an authentic but damaged painting by Francia that had undergone a 'complex and curious' restoration in the late nineteenth century.

Still, many questions remained. In 2009 the painting and its 'twin' in Pittsburgh were re-examined, existing data was re-assessed and new analyses undertaken. The X-radiographs taken of the National Gallery's painting in 1955 showed that channels left by woodworm, quite common in Italian poplar panels, had been filled with X-ray opaque material and thus appeared very light in the X-ray image. But the lack of exit holes on the back of the panel indicated that the channels had been filled from the front *before* the ground and paint layers had been applied. This led to the realisation that

the painting had been made on a 'recycled' old panel, planed down to receive a new painting. Such a phenomenon is found in paintings that have been transferred from one panel to another, as well as those deliberately made to appear deceptively old (case study 1). The unusual pink *imprimitura* was also reconsidered. Previously it had been excused by a similar priming layer in another painting by Francia in the National Gallery's collection. However, that painting had been transferred to a new panel probably in the eighteenth century. The coloured *imprimitura* seems to have been applied as part of the transfer process and was thus not original to Francia's painting. This realisation eliminated any possible argument to legitimise the coloured *imprimitura* in *The Virgin and Child with an Angel*.

The *imprimitura* in the Pittsburgh version is a more characteristic off-white colour.

In addition to the odd green pigment mixture called into question half a century earlier, new analysis revealed other pigments which would be unusual, if not impossible, for an authentic painting of the fifteenth century. A sample taken of the red curtain, for example, examined microscopically and with High Performance Liquid Chromatography (HPLC; p. 29) was found to contain a red lake pigment based on madder, of a type most probably manufactured in the nineteenth century. Other pigments identified include Naples yellow (lead-antimony yellow), usually found in paintings of a rather later date, and chrome yellow, a synthetic pigment commercially available from 1818.

Infrared reflectography (p. 23) revealed the underdrawing with greater clarity than was possible in the 1955 IR photograph. It appears to be executed in graphite pencil, based on a transfer from a pricked cartoon: some of the dots are still visible where they have not been joined up [38]. Visual identification of the medium presented an immediate anachronism, as graphite only came into use as a drawing material in the late sixteenth century. The underdrawing is unusually detailed, and in general more reminiscent of much later, finished drawings than authentic Renaissance underdrawings. In comparison, underdrawing in the Pittsburgh painting is executed in a liquid medium with a brush; it consists of very careful outlines combined with areas of diagonal hatching to indicate shadows. Although in general the Pittsburgh painting follows the underdrawn design with remarkable fidelity, infrared and X-ray images show that the artist made minor adjustments to the angel's profile as the work progressed.

In 1955 the National Gallery's restorer, Arthur Lucas, had noted the presence of 'pencil marks beneath the paint which could not have been made by an Italian Old Master'. In addition

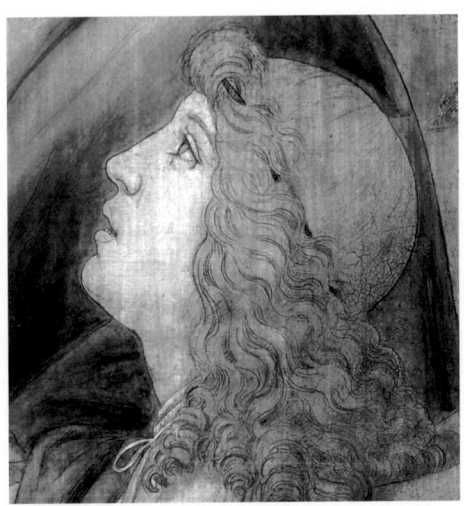

38. Infrared reflectogram of a detail of *The Virgin and Child with an Angel* (after Francesco Francia) showing the underdrawing for the angel's head, lower right.

to the pencil underdrawing described above, microscopic examination showed pencil lines applied on top of the paint in areas of fine detail, such as the child's hair, the trim of the Virgin's bodice and patterns on the chalice and on the angel's sleeve. This technique is uncharacteristic of Renaissance paintings (and no such pencil marks were found in the Pittsburgh painting), but has been observed in some nineteenth- and twentieth-century paintings.

We cannot be sure of the circumstances which prompted the creation of this skilful and highly convincing replica. But technical evidence suggests that it was made in Italy during the second half of the nineteenth century, by someone with an intimate knowledge of the original and some understanding of Italian Renaissance painting techniques. The re-use of an old wood panel and the meticulously applied 'cracks' suggest that it was made with a deliberate attempt to deceive.

CASE STUDY 3:
THE COPY AS HOMAGE

Attributed to Sassoferrato, after **Pietro Perugino**, *The Baptism of Christ*, about 1630–50

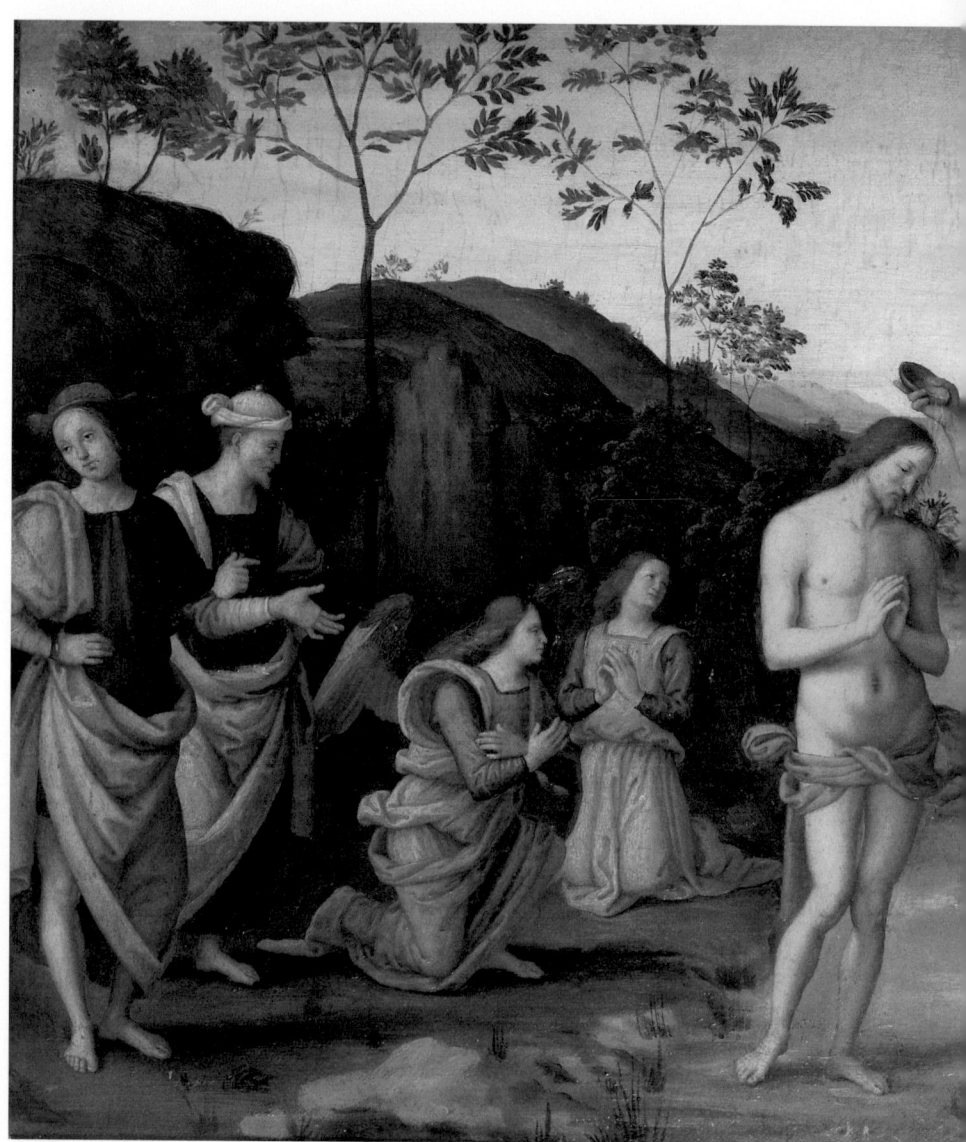

39. Attributed to Sassoferrato (1609–1685), after Pietro Perugino (living 1469; died 1523), *The Baptism of Christ*, about 1630–50, oil on canvas mounted on poplar, 32.5 x 59 cm.

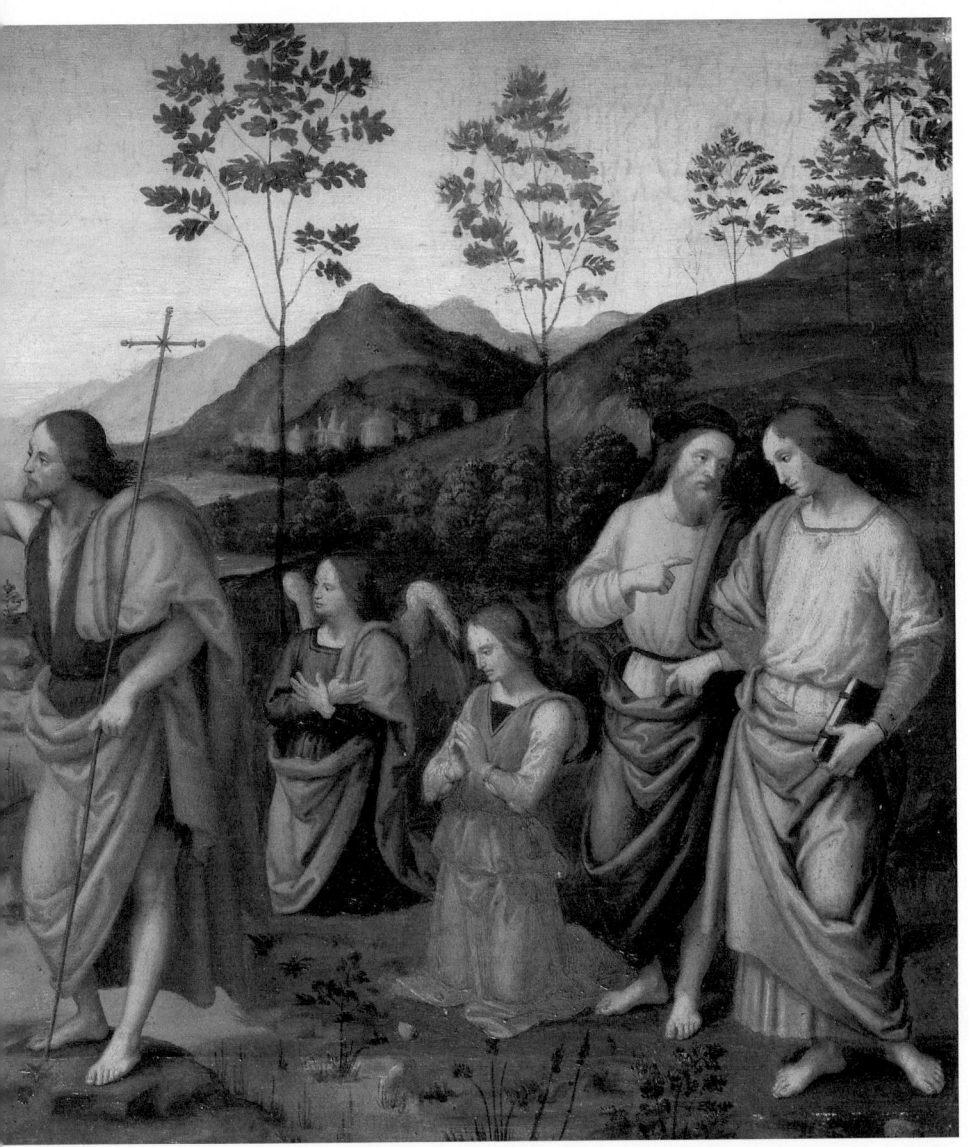

40. After Pietro Perugino (living 1469; died 1523), *The Baptism of Christ*, probably seventeenth century, oil on canvas mounted on wood, 32.5 x 59 cm. Canterbury City Council Museums (CANCM: 4030). Until recently, this painting was also thought to be a nineteenth-century copy. However, SEM–EDX analysis confirmed the presence of lead-tin-antimony yellow pigment, which had disappeared from use by the mid-eighteenth century. This suggests that this copy may also have been painted in the seventeenth century.

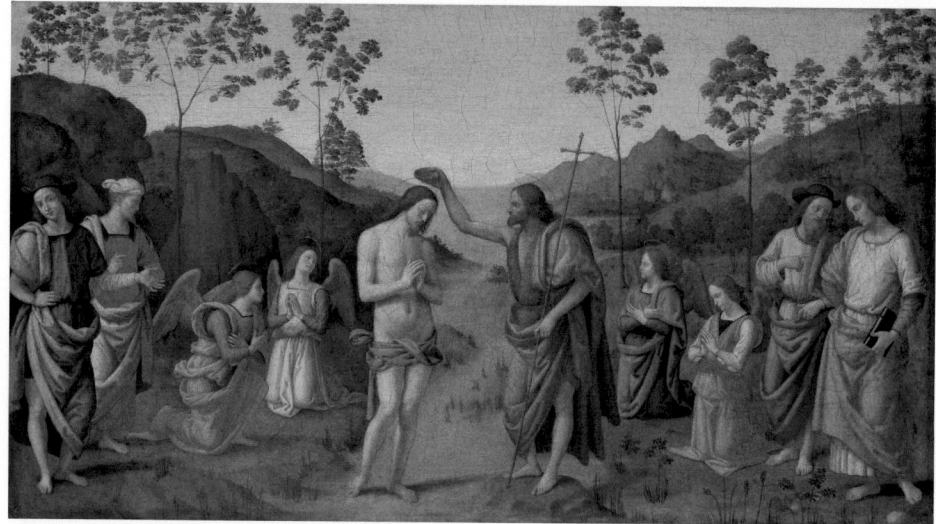

Distinguishing when, why, how, and by whom a copy was made can pose challenges for both scientist and art historian. *The Baptism of Christ* was purchased by the National Gallery in 1894 as 'ascribed to' Pietro Perugino – a qualification indicating a degree of doubt about an attribution to the master. More serious doubts about the picture were expressed within five years of its acquisition, when Herbert Horne, a prominent historian of Renaissance art, pronounced it 'not even a copy of the artist's own time, but of a period at least a hundred years later'. A full-blown scandal erupted in 1907, when the painting was denounced as a forgery painted in Florence in the first half of the nineteenth century. Further complicating matters was the existence of another, nearly identical version of the composition, which had been offered to the Gallery in 1887 but

declined; it was eventually acquired by the Royal Museum in Canterbury [40]. This, too, was labelled a modern forgery. Both paintings are indeed copies after Perugino, matching the original in scale and generally, though not precisely, in colour, but their histories are even more fascinating and complex.

The original painting by Perugino, now in the Musée des Beaux Arts in Rouen [41], formed part of the predella (base) of a large altarpiece commissioned for the high altar of the Benedictine Abbey of San Pietro in Perugia. It was completed in about 1500, but the ensemble was dismantled during a reorganisation of the church in 1591, and the small predella panels were removed to the sacristy. In the wake of Napoleonic campaigns into Italy at the end of the eighteenth century, both altarpiece and predella were transported to

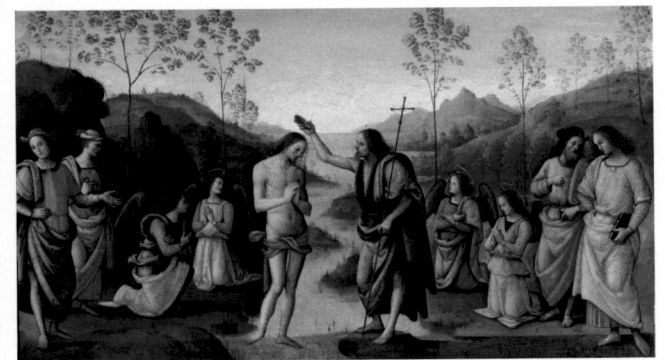

41. Pietro Perugino (living 1469; died 1523), *The Baptism of Christ*, about 1497, oil on wood, 39 x 68 cm. Musée des Beaux-Arts de Rouen (803–35)

France. The main altarpiece eventually found its way to Paris and the predella to Rouen, where it still resides.

Over the past century, the London version of *The Baptism of Christ* has periodically been the focus of scientific examination. Sampling and analysis done in 1970 led scientists to suspect that the painting might in fact be older than the nineteenth century. No modern blue pigments were detected, not even Prussian blue, known to have been available from 1704–10. Indeed, natural ultramarine (a mineral pigment extracted from lapis lazuli) was identified in the sky and azurite in the drapery. In addition, the ground used to prepare the canvas is pinkish-brown in colour; this is characteristic of paintings of the late sixteenth and early seventeenth centuries, but rare before and unusual after.

Further examinations were carried out in 2009 to refine the results of earlier investigations. These supported the idea that the painting was probably made during the seventeenth century. New evidence included identification of blue verditer (artificial azurite), a pigment which became common in the seventeenth century, in the dark green foliage at upper right. Azurite, a pigment rarely used after about 1700, was identified, combined with natural ultramarine in some areas of dark blue drapery. Even more revealing was the identification, by Raman microscopy [p. 26], of lead–tin–antimony yellow, since use of this pigment appears to have been most common to paintings of the seventeenth century which had some connection with Rome (case study 4).

But who might have painted the London *Baptism of Christ*? The fidelity of copy to original suggests that the copyist had access to Perugino's predella, which in the seventeenth century was still in the Benedictine Abbey of San Pietro in Perugia. One of the most highly regarded copyists of the seventeenth century (as well as an accomplished painter in his own right), Giovan Battista Salvi, called Sassoferrato, made a speciality of producing copies of sacred images. He is known to have painted several works (both original and reproductive) for the abbey, including enlarged copies after other panels from Perugino's altarpiece.

Apart from Sassoferrato's documented connection to the church, there are also convincing stylistic reasons for attributing the London *Baptism* to him. To the connoisseur, small deviations from the original reveal the particularities of the copyist's hand. In the copy, praying hands are clasped more loosely, as Sassoferrato was wont to do, and faces are fuller and rounder than Perugino's, with a sweetness entirely characteristic of the seventeenth-century painter. The leaves on the trees are also broader, almost as if they have been flattened against the surface; a similar effect is found in trees in the background of Sassoferrato's *Virgin and Child embracing*, also in the National Gallery.

CASE STUDY 4:
COPIES IN THE WORKSHOP

Angelo Caroselli, after **Nicolas Poussin**, *The Plague at Ashdod*, 1631

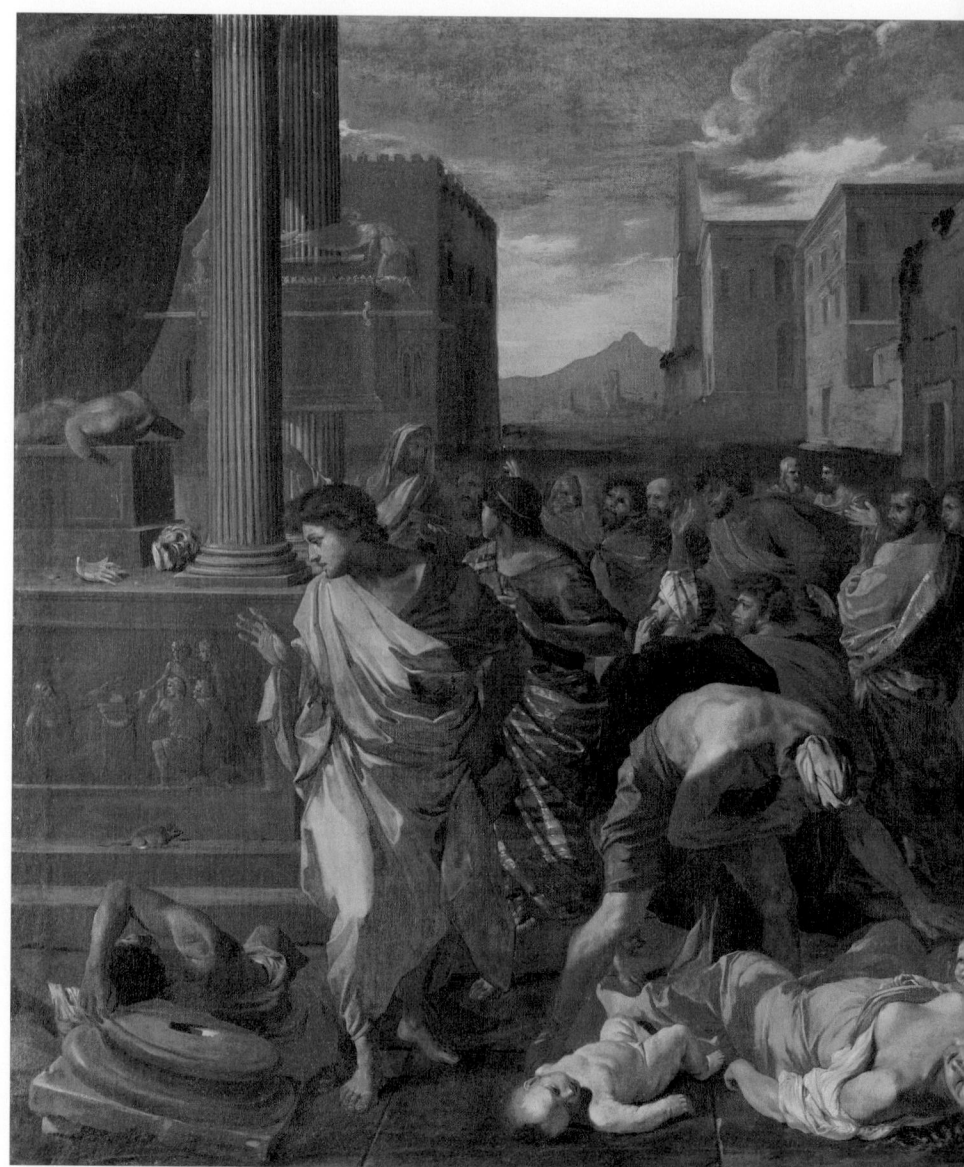

42. Angelo Caroselli (1585–1652), *The Plague at Ashdod* (after Poussin), 1631, oil on canvas, 129 x 204.5 cm.

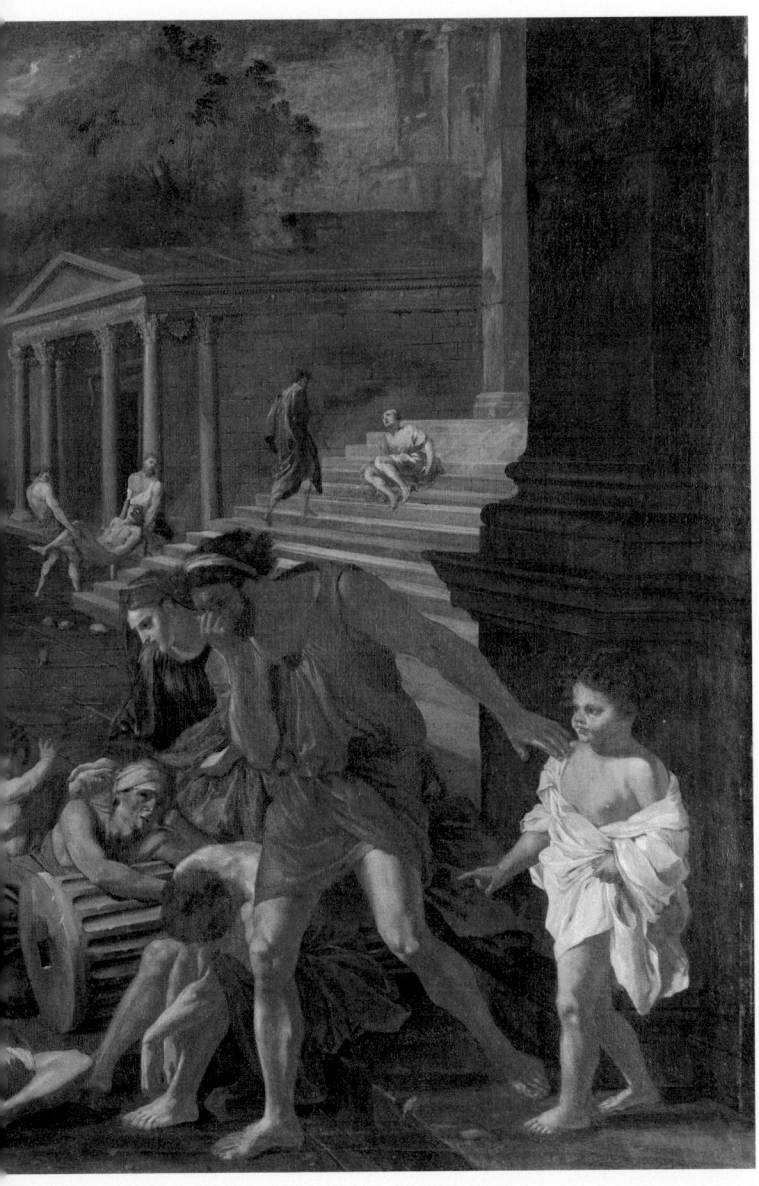

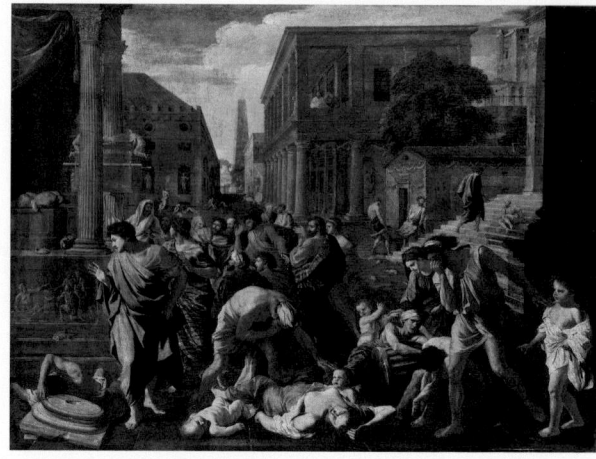

Right: 43. Nicolas Poussin (1594–1665), *The Plague at Ashdod*, 1631, oil on canvas, 148 x 198 cm. Musée du Louvre, Paris (7276).

Opposite page, left and right: 44, 45. Details of Angelo Caroselli (1585–1652), Nicolas Poussin (1594–1665), *The Plague at Ashdod*, 1631. In these black and white photographs, tracing lines in white lead are visible around some of the figures.

Caroselli's painting is an almost exact, and exactly contemporary, copy after Nicolas Poussin's *The Plague at Ashdod* of 1630/31 (43, now in the Musée du Louvre, Paris). The Sicilian nobleman Fabrizio Valguarnera acquired Poussin's original in February or March 1631, one of several paintings purchased in Rome with the spoils of a fabulous jewel heist. During a well publicised trial investigating the theft, in August 1631, Valguarnera testified that he had seen the painting in Poussin's studio while it was still unfinished. Valguarnera also commissioned Angelo Caroselli, a Roman painter, copyist and restorer, to make a copy of Poussin's painting. Both original and copy were in Valguarnera's possession by July 1631, but were probably sold soon after. The National Gallery's version was listed as a copy in seventeenth-century inventories, but by 1714 it was described as 'originale di Niccolò Pusino', and it was as an original by Poussin that it was presented to the National Gallery in 1838. In 1914 Otto Grauthoff, an expert on Poussin's work, published the painting as a second version of Poussin's *The Plague at Ashdod* in the Louvre, but it was not until the 1990s that the National Gallery's picture was once again connected with the copy made by Caroselli at Valguarnera's request.

It seems odd that Valguarnera would have possessed both original and copy of *The Plague at Ashdod*, but he apparently owned other such 'pairs', and may have anticipated selling one or the other. Caroselli was certainly considered a fair copyist in his day: the seventeenth-century artists' biographer Filippo Baldinucci reported that Poussin (notoriously disdainful of copyists) was himself deceived by a copy of a Raphael Madonna that Caroselli had painted. Caroselli seems to have worked directly from Poussin's original when composing his copy. Tracing lines in lead white are visible at the outlines of several of the principal figures in the foreground [44, 45], indicating that the painter had direct knowledge of Poussin's original. The lines were probably achieved by drawing the outlines of the figures on a sheet of fine translucent material placed over the original painting, then coating the back of the material with lead white. The material would then have been laid on top of a canvas prepared with a dark ground, and the outlines re-traced to transfer markings to the new canvas.

While the figures are repeated exactly from original to copy, the architectural settings are quite different. Infrared examination of the Louvre painting has shown that Poussin made considerable changes to the background

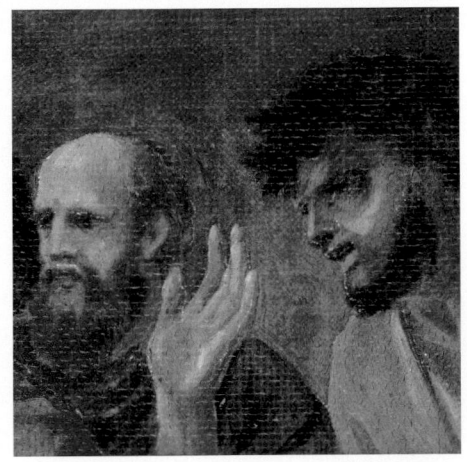 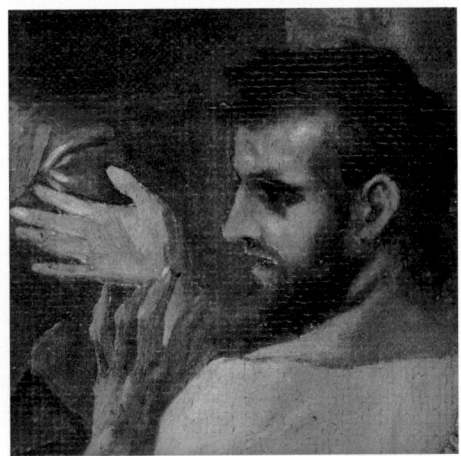

structures as he worked on the painting. It has been proposed that the National Gallery's picture was painted in Poussin's studio while the original was still unfinished, and that the difference in architectural details might document Poussin's earlier conception for the background of the Louvre picture. However, the architecture in Caroselli's version does not correspond to the preliminary designs in the Louvre painting. Perhaps Poussin had already altered the background of his painting by the time Caroselli came to paint this part of the composition and he was forced to rely on his memory of an earlier design; or perhaps the difference represents Carosselli's conscious attempt to personalise his copy of Poussin's original: early biographers praised Caroselli's ability to invent new compositions in the style of famous painters of the past and present.

The materials and techniques Caroselli employed are fairly common for seventeenth-century Italian paintings, with the exception of an opaque bright yellow used in the drapery of the figure wearing a striped toga. X-ray diffraction (XRD) analysis (p. 25) identified this as a lead-tin-antimony yellow — a pigment that seems to be relatively rare, but is most often found in paintings produced in Rome during the seventeenth century. As with paintings by Poussin, the balance of colours in Caroselli's painting has shifted due to increased transparency of the paint, colour change of unstable pigments and greater prominence of the dark ground. Smalt, for example (a blue pigment made from powdered glass coloured with cobalt oxide), has been used in a mixture with green earth in the foliage and landscape. Over the centuries the smalt has degraded, causing these areas to appear blanched and hazy, while increased transparency of the dark parts of the figures and their draperies has given the picture a rather sunken look.

CASE STUDY 5:
AMBITIOUS ATTRIBUTIONS

Attributed to Michiel Coxcie, *Portrait of a Man with a Skull*, about 1560 or later

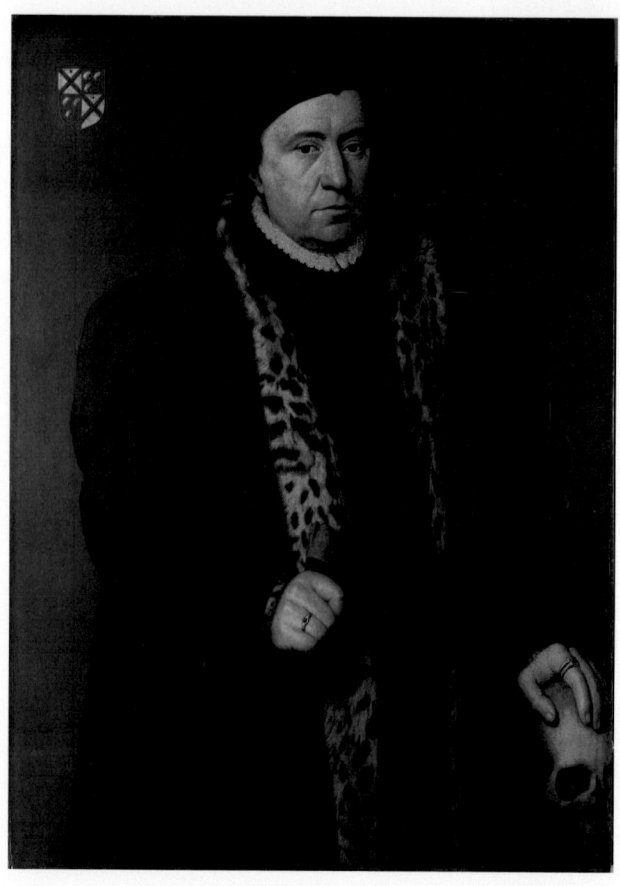

46. Attributed to Michiel Coxcie (1499–1592), *Portrait of a Man with a Skull*, about 1560 or later, oil on oak, 97.2 x 75.6 cm.

Rarely has a painting acquired with such fanfare fallen from favour so swiftly, or with such dramatic consequences. This portrait was purchased by the National Gallery in April 1845 for the substantial sum of £630, as a work by Hans Holbein the Younger. Holbein had worked in England in the 1520s, and again from 1532–43, and in the nineteenth century he was widely regarded as the first great British

artist. As this iconic painter was then not yet represented in the National Gallery's collection, the acquisition of a work by him was not only an institutional priority, but also an event of national significance.

From the moment this painting was installed in the Gallery, however, a cloud of suspicion surrounded it. Provoked by the less-than-prominent display accorded the new acquisition, one journalist remarked: 'Suspicious prudence hung it at such a height that no one without the aid of either a step-ladder, or great presumption, would dare to pronounce any decisive opinion upon it.' The painting's deficiencies were soon recognised: it lacked the assured draftsmanship and strong characterisation of the subject that distinguish a true Holbein. The dealer who had sold the 'Holbein' to the National Gallery admitted some doubt about who might have painted it, and the painting was temporarily removed from display. Newspaper accounts decried the scandalous expenditure of public money on a painting 'now vegetating in an inglorious obscurity'. Eventually the painting was quietly returned to view – but without its ambitious label. The Keeper responsible for the acquisition, Charles Lock Eastlake, was shattered by the scandal, and 'the Holbein affair' proved a major factor in his resignation barely two years later. (Eastlake did, however, later become the National Gallery's first director.)

When the National Gallery bought the portrait, it bore a spurious inscription at upper right: *I.* [or *J.*] *Holbein* /*1549*. As this inscription was visibly a later addition, it was removed. The attribution still seemed plausible enough, however, as Holbein's date of death was then believed to be 1554. Only in 1861 was Holbein's will discovered (in the archives of St Paul's Cathedral) which fixed the date of his death as 1543. In 1993, dendrochronological examination (p. 13) confirmed that Holbein could not possibly have painted the portrait. The painting's oak panel support is composed of three boards with the latest growth rings formed in 1542 and 1543. Allowing for trimmed sapwood rings, and for storage time to season the wood, the earliest possible date for the painting would be about 1554, although a date of 1560 or later is more likely – and well after Holbein's death.

Stripped of its prestigious 'Holbein' mantle, the *Portrait of a Man with a Skull* foundered without a firm attribution for more than a century and a half. It accumulated tentative and unconvincing suggestions, both Flemish and German painters. Unable to propose a definite artist for the portrait and perhaps overly mindful of the criticism heaped on the painting a century before, in 1945 National Gallery curator Martin Davies even suggested that it might be an early nineteenth-century fake. This is certainly not the case, however, as the dendrochronological date alone confirms; unlike the 'Francia' *Virgin and Child with an Angel* discussed in case study 2 (p. 39), there is no evidence that this is a later painting done on a 'recycled' panel.

The physical evidence, and the coat of arms at upper left, indicate that the painting was made in or near Brussels in about 1560.

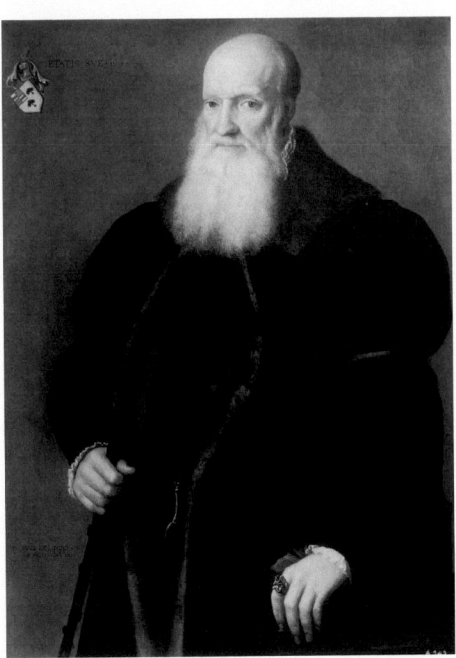

47. Michiel Coxcie (1499–1592), *Portrait of Gilles de Gottignies*, 1560, oil on oak, 111 x 80 cm. Formerly collection Comte de Brouchoven de Bergeyck, Antwerp (now lost).

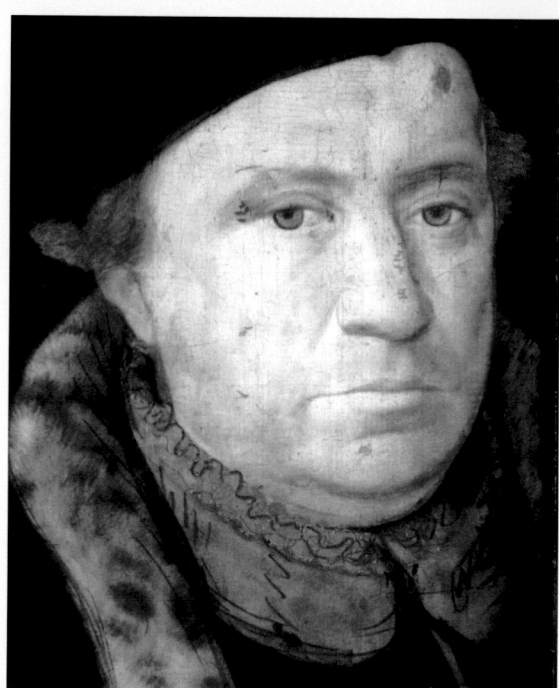

48. An infrared reflectogram of the sitter's head. The face has been drawn in a very clear, unelaborated manner, suggesting the artist might have transferred this from a drawing or cartoon. The collar exhibits a more vigorous freehand drawing technique.

Two portraitists of note were active in the city at that time, the more important being Michiel Coxcie, whose work in this field is not well known [47]. His portraits of the 1550s and 1560s are characterised by abrupt tonal transitions in the flesh, a uniform delineation of the upper and lower eyelids, and rather large, poorly drawn hands with stiff, sausage-like fingers – all of which are evident in the *Portrait of a Man with a Skull*. Infrared reflectograms [p. 23] reveal two types of underdrawing, both executed in a liquid medium applied with a brush. The head and facial features are simply and delicately drawn with no major changes, and may have been mechanically transferred from a study drawn on paper. The collar [48], hands and skull are sketched freehand in a much bolder style and show changes, especially in the hands and skull. The combination of two underdrawing techniques is not unusual in portraits of the sixteenth century (see case

study 8 for comparison). Future comparison of underdrawings in other portraits by Coxcie may help to confirm the proposed attribution.

The unknown man depicted in this portrait was initially believed to be a medical professor because of the skull at lower right, but this motif is commonly included in portraits of the sixteenth and seventeenth centuries as a *memento mori* (a pious reminder of mortality). Although the mere presence of a heraldic device, together with jewelled rings and expensive furred garments, would indicate a man of substantial means, he seems not to have followed the latest fashion trends: when the painting was created, in about 1560, most men wore beards and spotted furs had become outmoded. It was not unusual for older men and women to continue dressing in the styles of their youth, even long after they had passed from fashion. It is hoped that ongoing research into the coat of arms will yield a more precise identification of the sitter.

CASE STUDY 6:
FINDING GIORGIONE

Giorgione, *Il Tramonto (The Sunset)*, 1506–10

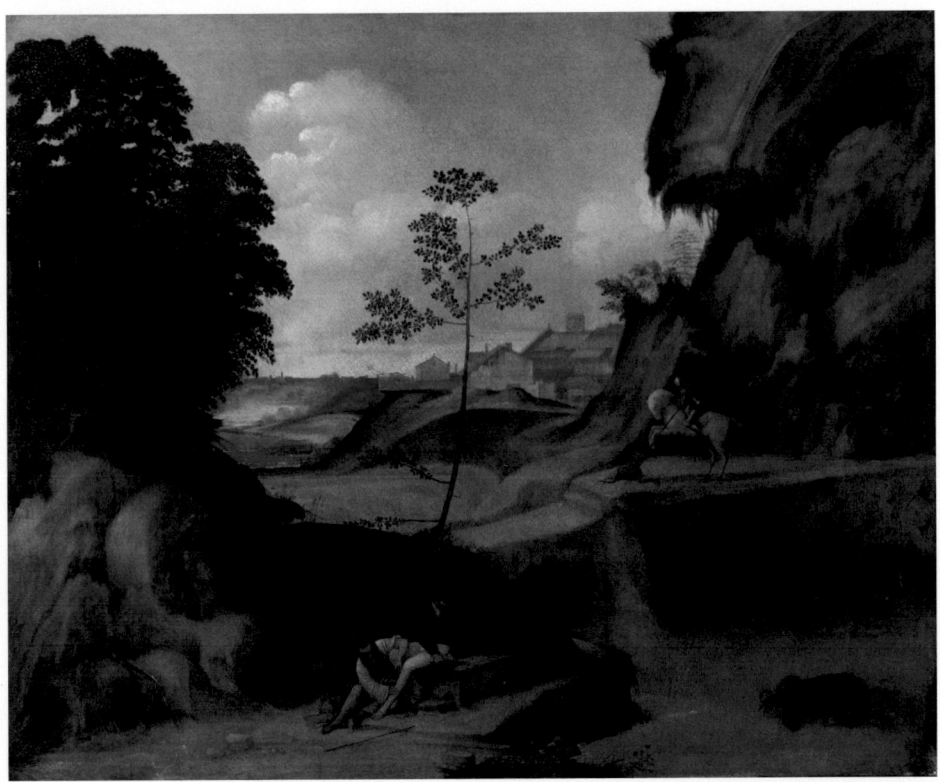

For many years the National Gallery sought to round out its superb collection of Venetian paintings with a work by Giorgione, Titian's mentor and one of the most elusive and enigmatic of Renaissance masters. In 1937 Kenneth Clark, the Gallery's young director, persuaded the Trustees to acquire the elegiac *Scenes from Tebaldeo's Eclogues*, now attributed to Andrea Previtali. Clark considered the paintings to be close to Giorgione and perhaps by him, but the Trustees persuaded him to claim more definitively that they were by the artist [50]. The purchase of these paintings, immediately rejected as possible Giorgiones by all scholars in the field, triggered a scandal comparable to that surrounding the purchase of the 'Holbein' a century earlier (case study 5).

The controversy left a lingering stain, and when another opportunity arose to acquire a painting by Giorgione, in the 1950s, the Gallery understandably proceeded with extreme caution. Even decades later, as one writer noted, 'the bitterness of the controversy over the little pictures [the *Eclogues*] … is weighing much

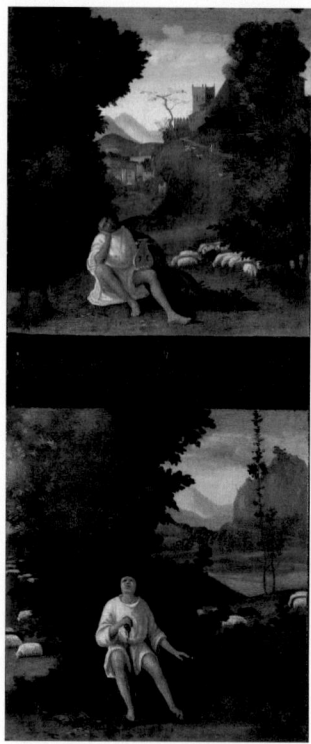
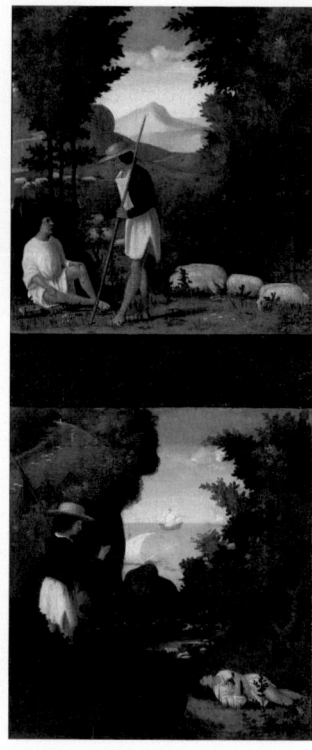

Previous page: 49.
Giorgione (active 1506;
died 1510), *Il Tramonto
(The Sunset)*, 1506–10, oil
on canvas, 73.3 x 91.4 cm.

Right: 50. Andrea Previtali
(about 1480–1528), *Scenes
from Tebaldeo's Eclogues:
The Story of Damon*,
perhaps about 1505, oil on
wood, 45.2 x 19.9 cm.

Opposite page: 51.
Il Tramonto (The Sunset),
1506–10, shortly after its
discovery in 1933.

Overleaf: 52. Detail of 49.

too strong…'. Efforts to procure the 'new'
Giorgione commenced in 1957, but only
came to a successful conclusion in 1961.

The painting in question, *Il Tramonto
(The Sunset)*, had been discovered only in 1933.
Found neglected in a storeroom in the Villa
Garzoni, near Padua, it appeared to be in quite
desperate condition [51]. Photographs taken
at the time – under raking light (p. 21), which
accentuates the impression of damage – show
losses of paint and of canvas in the trees at
the left, and in the foreground area to the right.
Yet the centre of the picture, and especially the
distant landscape view, were quite well preserved
and the painting was recognised (initially by
the art critic Giorgio Sangiorgi) as an authentic
Giorgione. The Florentine restorer Augusto
Vermehren superficially cleaned the painting,
lined the fragile canvas, patched holes with what
appear to be scraps of old canvas, and repainted

areas of loss. Photographs of the painting at
this stage of restoration do not include the
figure of the horseman at right or the figure in
the cave at far right; the lower right foreground
also appears undefined. In 1934, following the
sale of *Il Tramonto* to the collector-dealer Vitale
Bloch, the painting was again restored, this time
in Rome by Theodor Dumler. Vermehren's
repaint was removed, revealing the figure in
the cave, as well as the haunches and double
tail of the 'dragon'. Dumler may also have
been responsible for introducing the figure
on horseback that now confronts the 'dragon'.
Dark shapes in the watery area at lower right
were reconstructed as three distinct rocks, and
the entire painting covered with a heavily
toned varnish.

When the National Gallery acquired
the painting in 1961, it was partially cleaned
and restored once more by the Gallery's

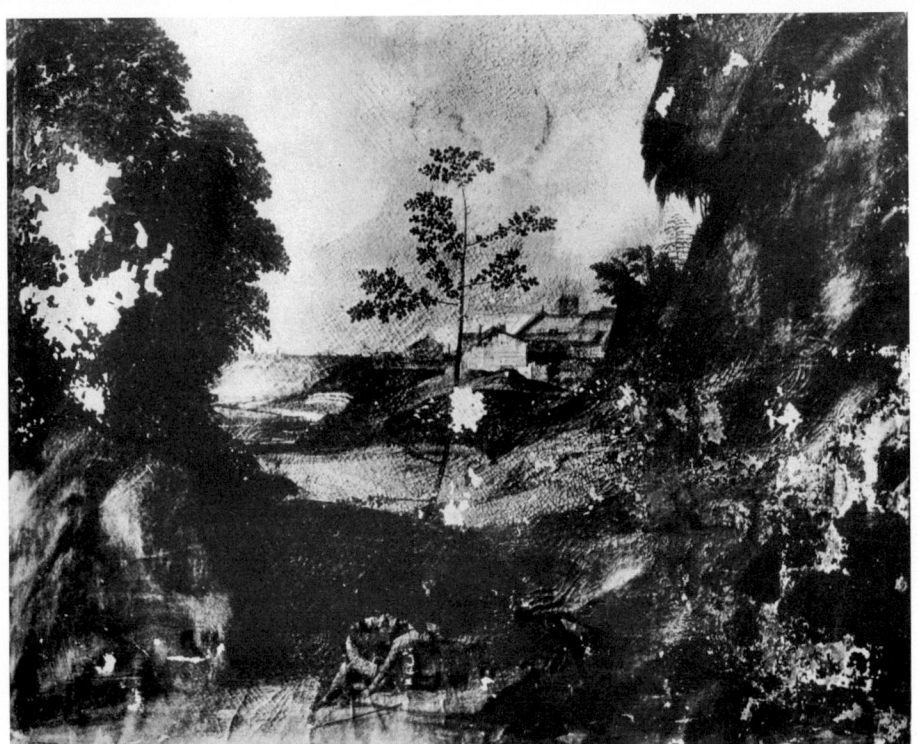

restorer Arthur Lucas. He emphasised the anthropomorphic qualities of the dark forms in the water at lower right and delineated the figure of horse and rider more boldly, to give it greater prominence in the composition. The bright blue of the saddle cloth (which in fact derives from a piece of the previously painted canvas patch and is not original to Giorgione's painting) now forms an important colour accent within the composition. The present mottled appearance of the pond bank may result from Lucas's imperfect understanding of the previous reconstruction of this damaged area.

Because they have affected a few small but telling details within the composition, the successive restorations of *Il Tramonto* have profoundly influenced the interpretation of this mysterious painting. The figure in the cave at far right, which appears to be original, has been identified as Saint Anthony Abbot, and the 'monsters' in the water below as the nightmarish hybrid creatures that tormented him. Many have seen in these creatures (some of which are original) the influence of the Netherlandish painter Hieronymus Bosch's fantastical beasts. The mounted figure has been read as Saint George, and the two men in the foreground, more problematically, as a plague-stricken Saint Roch, assisted by Gothardus. Individually and collectively the identification of the figures is problematic, not least because some of the salient details are necessarily conjectural restorations which may not accurately reflect Giorgione's original intent. Indeed, the artist may not have meant this lyrical landscape to have a biblical or narrative subject at all. Present understanding of the painting would suggest that the more evocative and open-ended title of *Il Tramonto* is, for now, at least, the most appropriate.

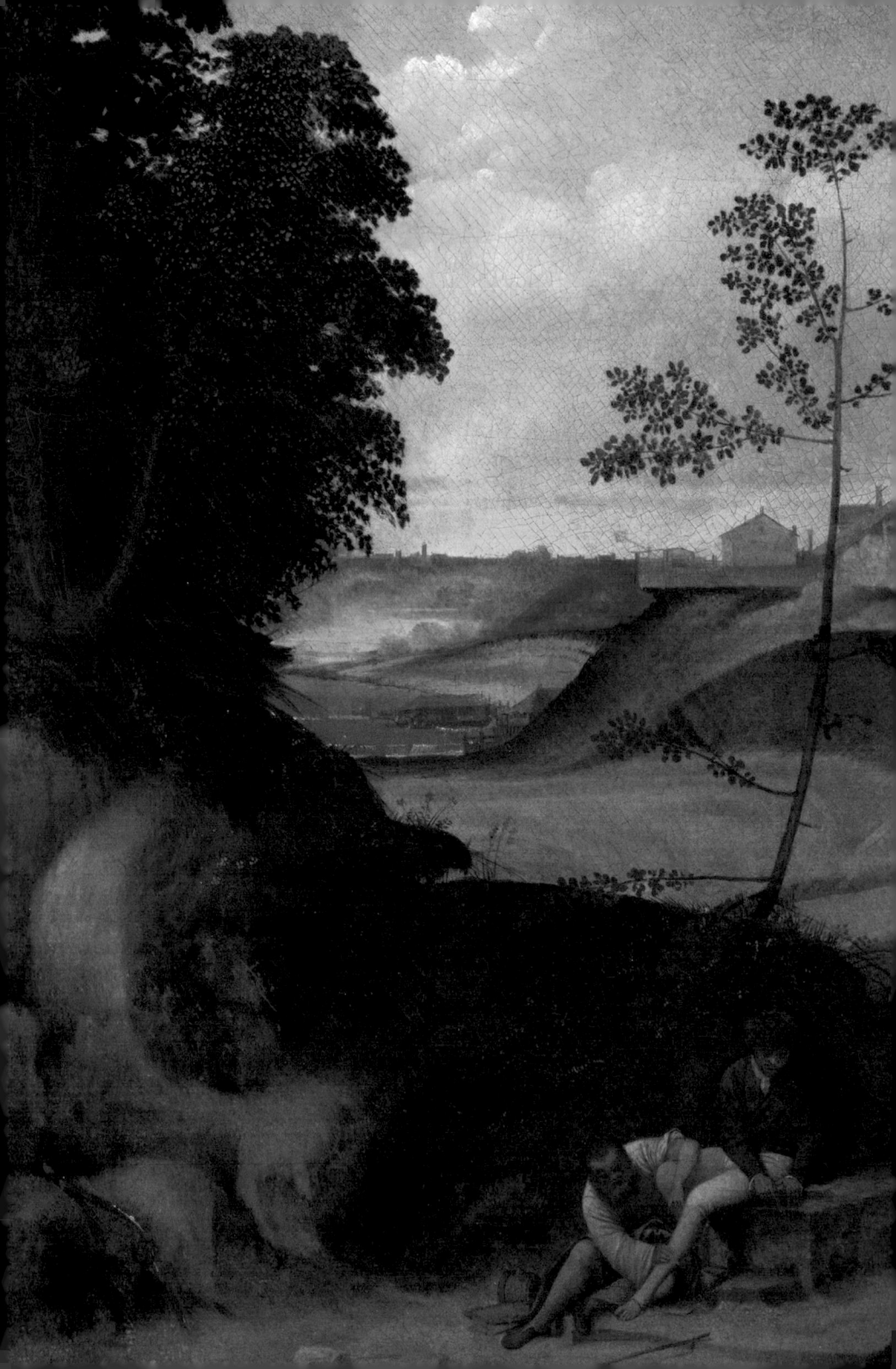

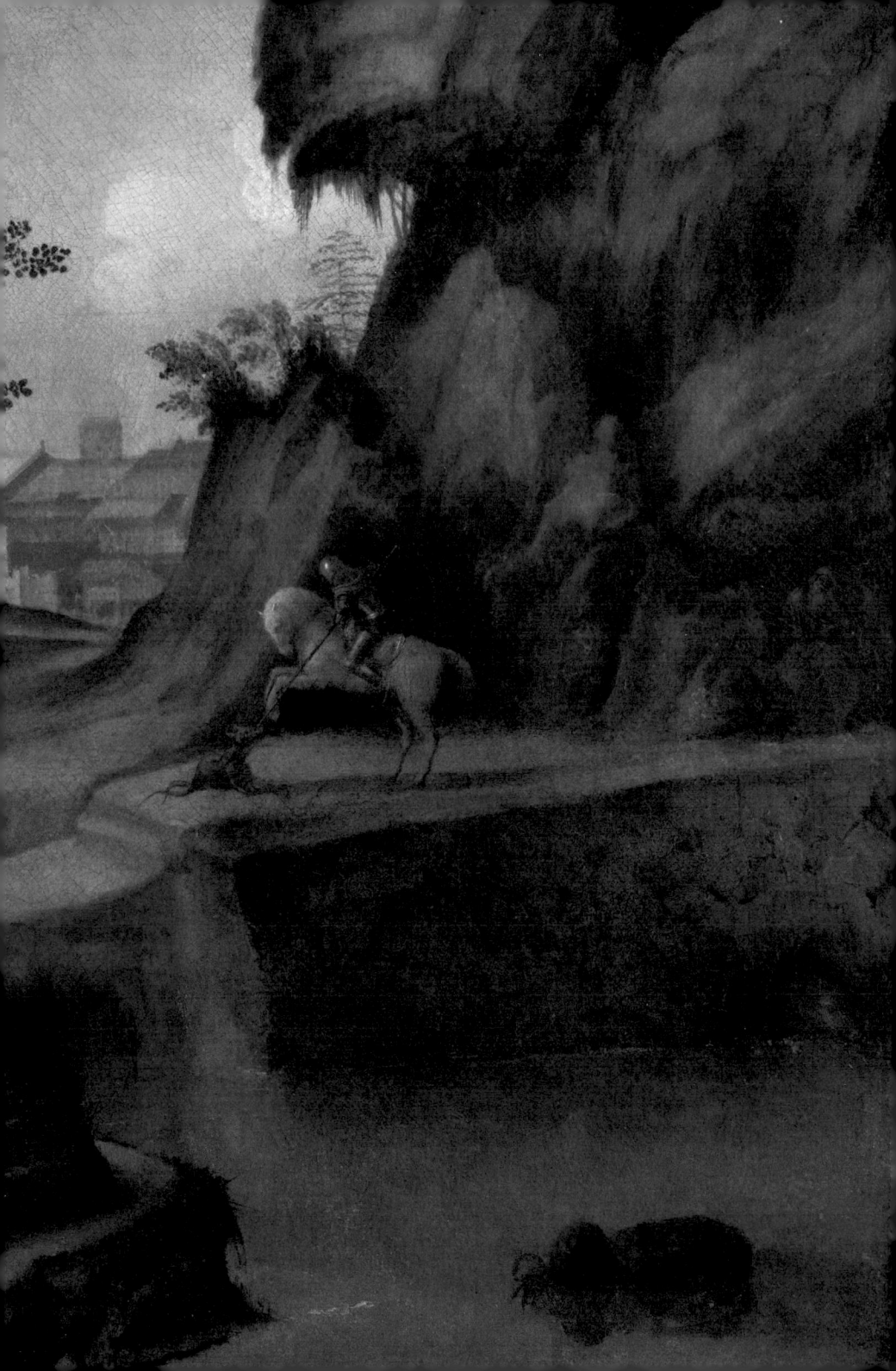

CASE STUDY 7:
REMBRANDT'S WORKSHOP

Follower of Rembrandt, *An Old Man in an Armchair*, 1650s

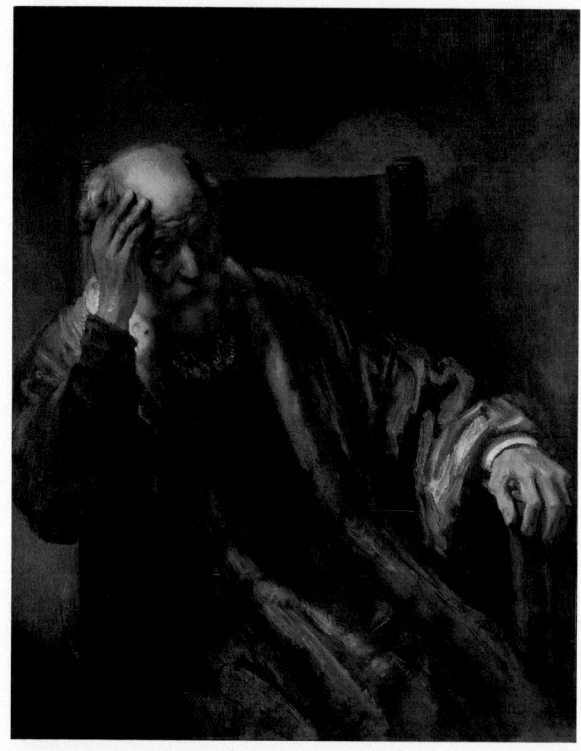

53. Follower of Rembrandt
(1606–1669), *An Old Man in*
an Armchair, 1650s,
oil on canvas, 111 x 88 cm.

Half a century ago, when the National Gallery acquired this painting, it was praised as a powerful example of Rembrandt's work of the 1650s. Several art historians, most notably Sir Kenneth Clark, remarked on the pronounced 'Venetian' aspect of the painting, citing the pure, saturated colours and the use of glazes to create depth of tone. Clark also suggested that the composition might be Rembrandt's 'reminiscence of a Tintoretto portrait', though no specific prototype was cited and indeed Rembrandt may not have known the work of the Venetian master. By the late 1960s, a more

systematic comparison of *An Old Man in an Armchair* with authentic works by Rembrandt, coupled with a greater understanding of the materials and techniques used in paintings by Rembrandt and artists in his circle, enabled scholars to recognise the painting as the work of a contemporary follower.

An Old Man in an Armchair is superficially convincing as a work by Rembrandt. The subject of an old man in contemplation was a common theme in his oeuvre. The painting also bears a signature and date (1652) at upper right – although this is false. Moreover there

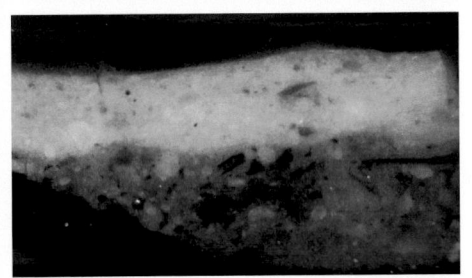

54. Cross-section of a paint sample from *An Old Man in an Armchair*, taken from the sitter's proper left hand. It shows the use of a red lake glaze over a cream underpaint. The double ground is visible beneath.

are aspects of quality, technique and handling of paint that find no parallel in the master's work. There is a conspicuous, almost jarring disparity of style between the loose handling of the beard, fur coat and proper right hand and the man's left hand and sleeve, which are rendered in an almost impressionistic manner. The noted 'Venetian' effect results largely from the use of comparatively pure pigments: the bright red on the man's proper left cuff is pure vermilion, the orange-yellow streaks in his robe are just natural earth pigment, and the deep purplish glazes consist solely of red lake (organic dye) pigments. This use of red lake glazes on the sitter's gown and on his hand would be most unusual in authentic paintings by Rembrandt of this period [54].

The painting cannot simply be dismissed as a later imitation, however, as the materials used suggest that it was produced either in Rembrandt's studio during the 1650s or by a contemporary painter emulating something of Rembrandt's style. The canvas was prepared with a double ground typical of Dutch seventeenth-century practice. It consists of a lower layer of orange-red earth pigment and a second, irregular layer of a dull brownish-olive colour containing lead white, wood charcoal and some yellow ochre (pigments identified microscopically and by EDX, p.25). Although double grounds are common, they vary considerably in their exact constitution. The fact that rather similar grounds are found in Rembrandt's portraits of Jacob Trip and Margaretha de Geer of about 1660, both owned by the National Gallery, suggests that *An Old Man in an Armchair* may also have originated in Rembrandt's studio. The grounds for all these pictures seem to have been applied in the studio rather than the canvases having been commercially primed: many of the specific pigments found in the ground layers have also been identified in the paint itself. Moreover, in examining cross-sections under the microscope, the interface between the two ground layers can be seen to merge together, suggesting that each layer had not yet completely dried before the next was applied. These technical features have been identified in several autograph paintings by Rembrandt.

But who might have painted *An Old Man in an Armchair*? We are reasonably well informed about the many painters active in Rembrandt's studio during the course of his career, but less confident about specific aspects of their training. It seems that pupils were encouraged not just to copy the master's work as a way of learning from it, but also to create independent paintings inspired by motifs or themes borrowed from Rembrandt. Before they became master painters in their own right (see p. 60), guild regulations prohibited pupils from signing their works, and some of their better efforts may have been provided with the master's signature before leaving the studio. A convincing author has yet to be found for this evocative painting of an old man immersed in thought. Careful connoisseurship and continued scientific investigation of works by Rembrandt and his followers may one day solve the puzzle.

CASE STUDY 8:
WORKSHOP COLLABORATION

Andrea del Verrocchio with the assistance of **Lorenzo di Credi**,
The Virgin and Child with Two Angels, about 1476–8

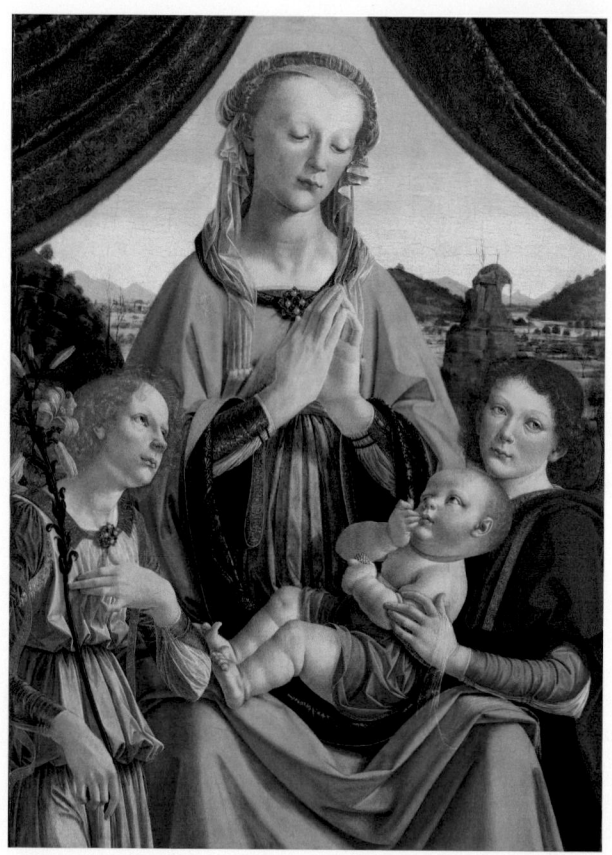

55. Andrea del Verrocchio (about 1435–1488) with the assistance of Lorenzo di Credi (about 1458–1537), *The Virgin and Child with Two Angels*, about 1476–8, tempera on wood, 96.5 x 70.5 cm.

The productions and working practices of artistic workshops pose a particular challenge both to connoisseurship and technical analysis. Subject to guild regulations, a master painter – or sculptor, craftsman or architect – might employ any number of pupils and assistants to aid in all aspects of producing a work of art. Although activities within the studio were overseen by the master, it did not necessarily only produce works exclusively by his hand. On the contrary, several levels of cooperative practice might exist within an individual studio. The master might be responsible for the entire design and execution of a work; a work might be designed by the master but executed wholly or in part by assistants; or it might be inspired by works by the master but actually designed and executed entirely by his assistants. All of

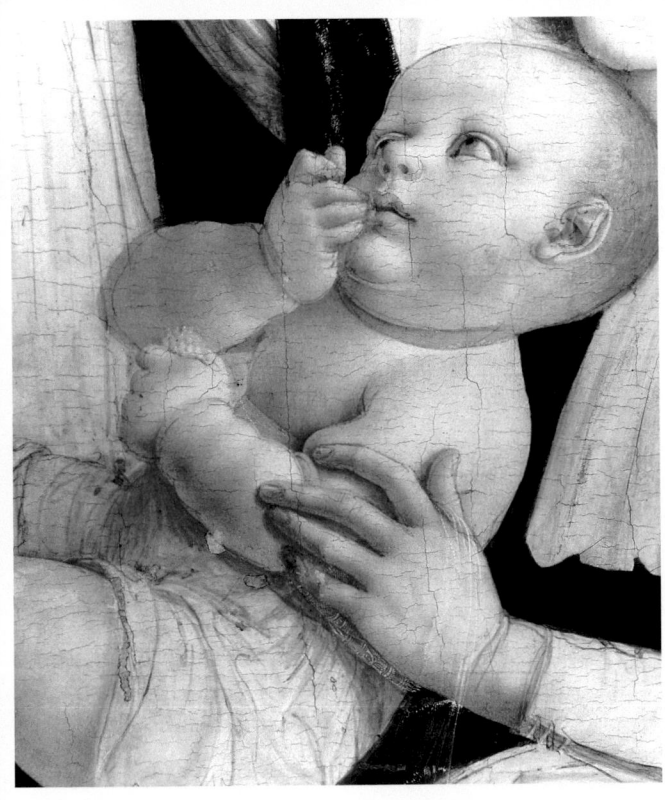

56. The infrared reflectogram of *The Virgin and Child with Two Angels* reveals extensive underdrawing and pouncing (detail).

these can legitimately be described as products of the master's workshop.

Perhaps the most fertile artistic workshop operating in Florence during the 1470s was that of Andrea del Verrocchio. An accomplished painter, sculptor, goldsmith and draughtsman, Verrocchio provided training to some of the most gifted artists of the Renaissance, including the young Leonardo da Vinci. He organised the activities of his studio quite strictly in order to maintain a reliable and recognisable standard of production. The quality and efficiency of his workshop were doubtless appreciated by clients, but these same characteristics have made it extremely difficult for modern researchers to identify the contributions of different 'hands' in the production of a work. To achieve a harmonious whole, each artist largely suppressed distinctive individual stylistic or technical traits.

Moreover, as no signed paintings by Verrocchio are known, reconstructing his actual production remains a matter of considerable debate.

One of the most finely executed paintings to have survived from the Verrocchio workshop, *The Virgin and Child with Two Angels* was acquired by the National Gallery in 1857 as a work by Domenico Ghirlandaio, a Florentine artist who probably trained with Verrocchio. The painting had previously been described as a work by Piero della Francesca, and subsequent attributions have ranged from Pollaiuolo to the young Perugino, or to various other Florentine artists active in the 1470s. While scholars now agree that the painting was made in the Verrocchio studio, there has been little consensus as to who within the workshop might have contributed to the execution, or whether Verrocchio himself had a hand in it.

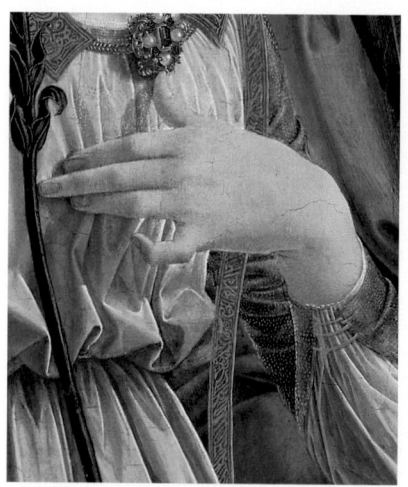 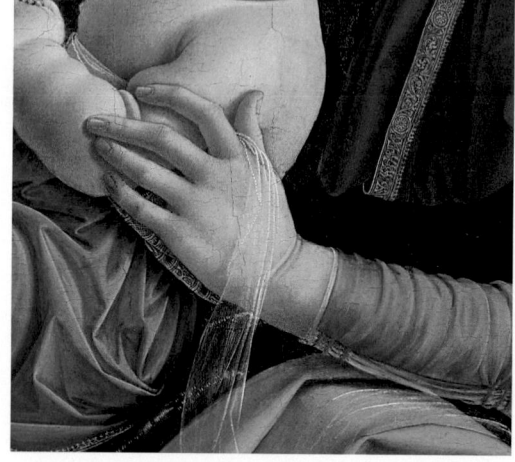

Unfortunately scientific analysis cannot help in this instance, as investigations have shown that the painting's materials and technique are entirely consistent throughout. However, recent cleaning and restoration, removing three centuries of disfiguring retouches, has emphasised the painting's extraordinary refinement and allowed more accurate assessment of its execution.

Infrared reflectograms revealed extensive underdrawing (p. 22). The heads, hands, and baby all show evidence of pouncing, a method of transferring a design by dabbing a pricked drawing with powdered charcoal or chalk to produce a series of dots on the surface below [56]. While these elements of the design were transferred from existing drawings, the remainder of the composition is underdrawn freehand. The composition itself seems more an assemblage of individual parts than a unified design: the angel on the right occupies no real position in space and the child floats, awkwardly wedged between the head of the angel on the right and the elbow of the angel on the left.

The work appears to have been painted by two artists, one responsible for the infant Christ and the angel at the right; the other for the Virgin, the landscape, and the angel at the left. A comparison of the angels' hands shows the difference between the two quite clearly [57, 58]. The ones on the left are fragile and almost painfully elegant, with a clear sense of the underlying tendons and veins. In comparison, the one on the right seems flaccid, the artist adopting a heightened contrast of highlight and shadow in an attempt to evoke rounded forms. This way of modelling forms, as well as details such as the baby's turned-up toes, is entirely characteristic of Lorenzo di Credi, one of Verrocchio's leading assistants during the 1470s. The expressive beauty and subtle handling of the other angel, however, finds its closest parallel in drawings and sculptures by Verrocchio himself. So compelling are these comparisons, in fact, that *The Virgin and Child with Two Angels* may well become a touchstone for future attributions to the elusive painter Verrocchio.

CASE STUDY 9:
WORKING PROCESS I

Lorenzo Lotto, *Portrait of a Woman inspired by Lucretia*, about 1530–2

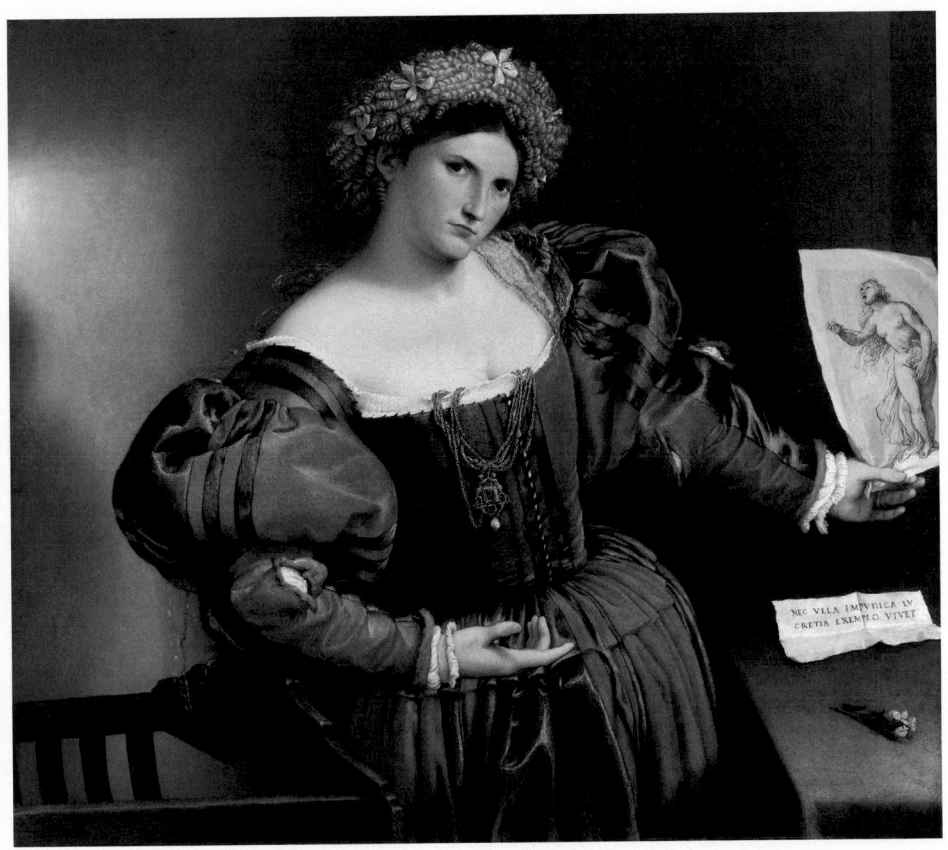

59. Lorenzo Lotto (about 1480–1556/7),
Portrait of a Woman inspired by Lucretia,
about 1530–2, oil on canvas, 96.5 x 110.6 cm.

Beneath the surface of many paintings in the National Gallery lie traces of revisions introduced by the artist as he worked – some quite minor, others more extensive. When X-ray and infrared photographs were made of Lorenzo Lotto's *Portrait of a Woman inspired by Lucretia* in 1998, it was discovered that the artist made some surprisingly dramatic changes to the background as he painted.

63

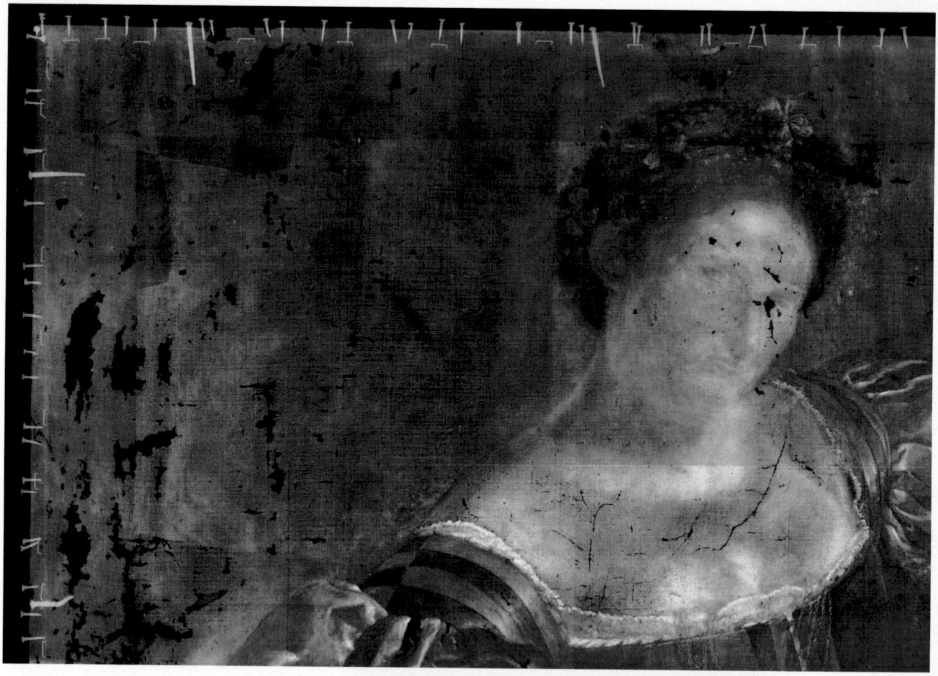

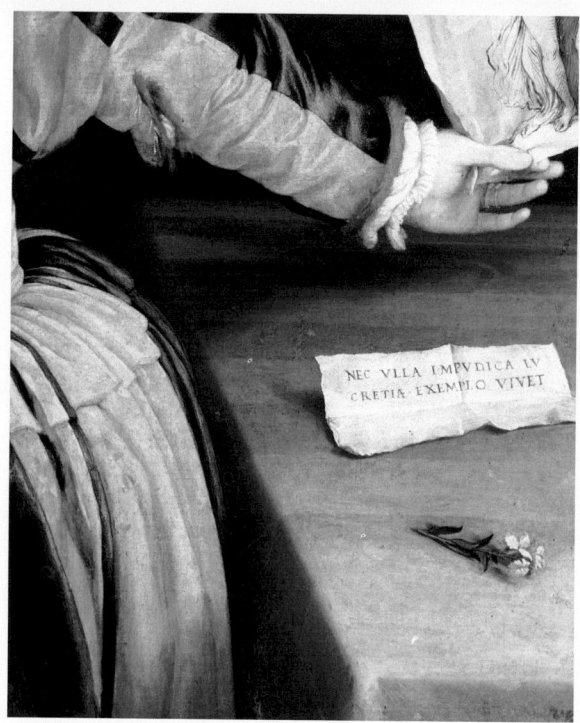

Above: 60. Detail of X-radiograph of *Portrait of a Woman inspired by Lucretia*.

Right: 61. Detail of infrared photograph of *Portrait of a Woman inspired by Lucretia*. The blue stripes on the tablecloth (horizontal) and in the background (vertical) appear light in the X-radiograph but dark in the infrared photograph. This is due to the use of azurite, which absorbs both X-ray and infrared radiation.

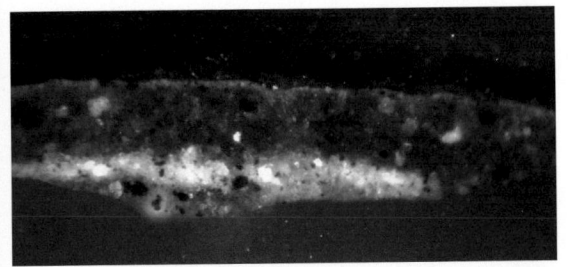

62. Cross-section from the background of *Portrait of a Woman inspired by Lucretia,* showing the initial layer of a blue colour (azurite) in a now-concealed stripe.

Portraits by Lotto are typically bold, innovative and highly individual; he often chose a horizontal format to accommodate symbolic elements and the expansive gestures of his figures. This compelling portrait of an unknown woman was purchased by the National Gallery in 1927. As the woman holds a drawing of the virtuous Roman matron Lucretia, this may be her name as well. However, it is also possible that she holds the drawing to indicate her commitment to a similarly virtuous path.

The woman's fashionable gown, alternating broad panels and narrower bands of bright green and orange, makes a striking statement. X-ray and infrared photographs [60, 61] showed that Lotto originally situated this figure not against the neutral grey we now see, but against a background of broad vertical stripes, possibly simulating a textile or painted decoration. Guided by the X-ray and infrared images, paint samples were taken to discover what colours lay beneath the surface. Microscopic examination of the cross-sections revealed stripes of blue (azurite mixed with lead white [62]), alternating with pink (red lake, lead white and a little vermilion) shading to mauve (red lake, azurite and lead white). The images also clearly showed that the tablecloth was horizontally striped – analysis of paint samples taken from

this area indicate that it was initially a light greyish-blue with mauve. Because the paint of the woman's dress overlaps the grey of the present background in some areas, it would appear that Lotto obliterated the patterned background at quite an early stage. In contrast, hints of blue pigment can still be seen at the edges of the paper and sprig of wallflowers on the table, indicating that the stripes here were only covered over *after* these details were painted.

One other change that Lotto made has become partly visible even to the naked eye. Beneath the representation of an ink drawing of Lucretia on the paper held by the sitter is a coloured image of a woman. Presumably also a Lucretia, her head is lower down and faces in the opposite direction, and her left arm is raised. This earlier version seems to show a drawing done on a smaller sheet of blue paper. Increased transparency of the upper layer of white paint (an effect of age) has slowly unmasked the artist's reworking of this detail. The X-ray image revealed that this change was probably done quite quickly: the main lines of the drawing were painted onto the white paint of the paper while it was still wet, displacing the paint and creating thinner areas that register as dark marks in the X-radiograph.

CASE STUDY 10:
WORKING PROCESS II

Pierre-Auguste Renoir, *The Umbrellas (Les Parapluies)*, about 1881–6

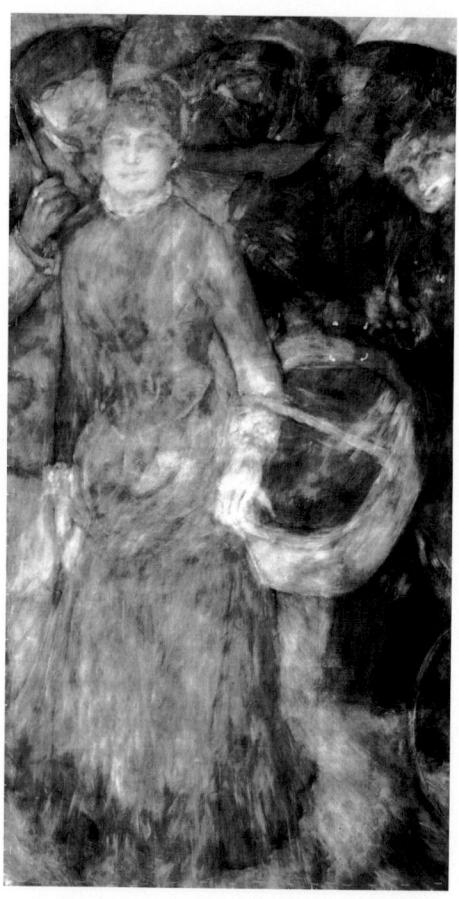

Above: 63. This detail of the X-radiograph of
The Umbrellas shows extensive changes made
to the costume of the woman on the left.

Opposite page: 64.
Pierre-Auguste Renoir (1841–1919),
The Umbrellas, about 1881–6, oil on canvas,
180.3 x 114.9 cm.

Many of the physical transformations revealed
in the course of a technical examination shed
light on the artist's reworking of compositional
details or rethinking of iconographic strategies.
On occasion, however, such analyses can provide
insight into a painter's stylistic evolution and
changing approach to his craft.

During the 1880s Renoir became
increasingly anxious about the nature and
ambition of his art. As he later confided to the
art dealer and patron Ambroise Vollard:
'I had come to the end of Impressionism, and
I was reaching the conclusion that I didn't
know how either to paint or draw. In a word,
I was at a dead end.' At the crux of Renoir's
dilemma was whether luminous surfaces and
diffuse brushwork – hallmarks of Impressionist
technique and so well suited to the *plein-air*
landscapes he had painted earlier in his career –
were in fact appropriate to the figure paintings
and portraits that had come to play a larger
role in his work, and which seemed to demand
greater structure and clarity of form.

Born of this time of restless experimentation,
Renoir's *The Umbrellas* displays two very
different styles of painting. The figures on
the right are painted using a palette of vibrant
colours applied in a soft, feathery style
reminiscent of Renoir's Impressionist work of
the late 1870s [66]. However, the umbrellas and
the figures on the left are painted in a harder,
more linear manner, using more subdued
colours [65]. Stylistic analysis, together with an
early X-ray photograph [63], established that
the composition we now see was painted in
two distinct stages – the figures on the right

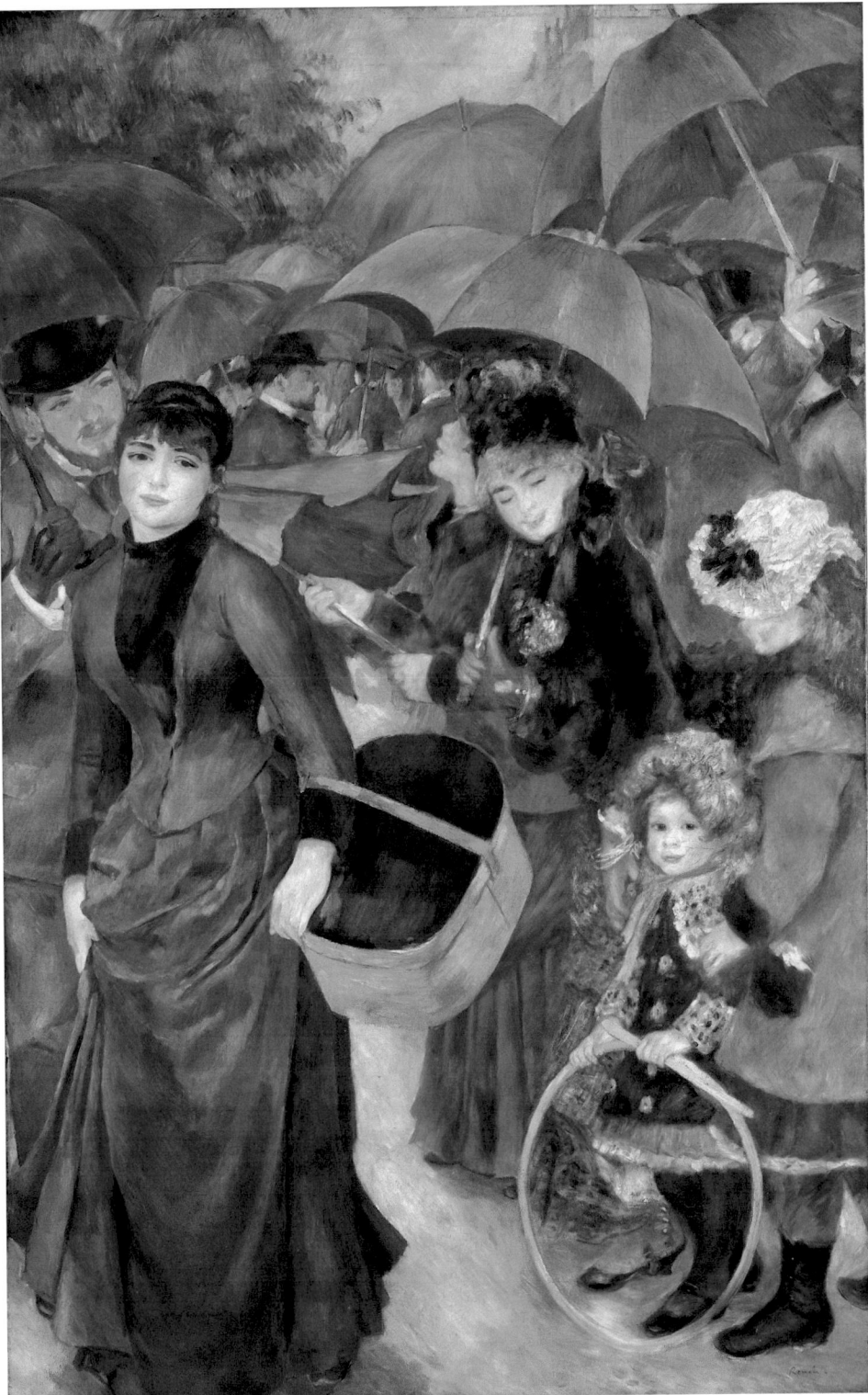

65, 66. Pierre-Auguste Renoir (1841–1919),
The Umbrellas, about 1881–6. The faces of these
two woman depicted in *The Umbrellas* show the
contrasting styles of painting that Renoir applied
in the work.

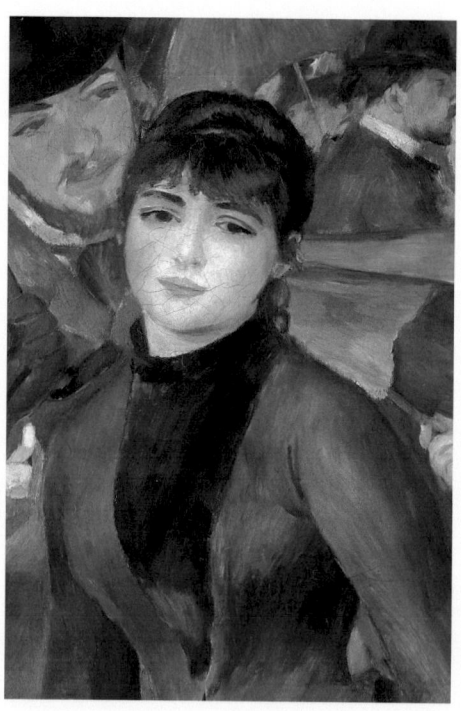 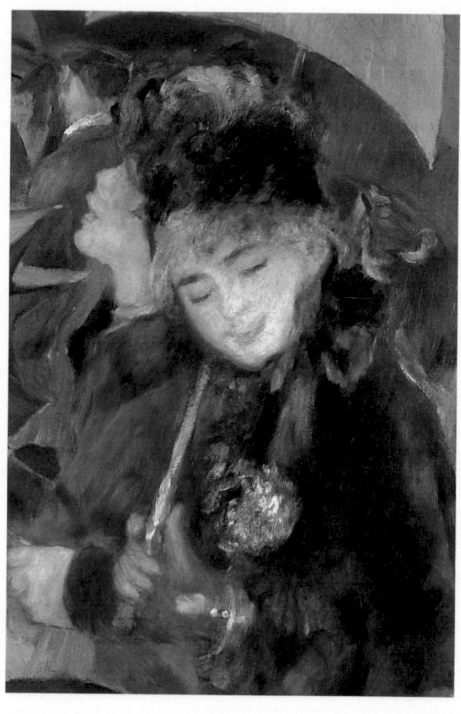

probably in about 1881 and the remainder of
the painting in about 1885–6. The women's
costumes confirm the proposed dating. Dresses
and hats worn by the right-hand figures exhibit
the frilly, feminine styles popular in 1881, while
the simpler, more severe costume worn by
the woman on the left represented the height
of fashion in 1885–6.

Only comparatively recently, with the aid
of technical investigations carried out in the
1980s, has the evolution of this complex picture
been more fully understood. The X-ray image
shows little change to the group of figures on
the right, but substantial changes to the figure
of the woman on the left. Renoir seems to have

first painted the entire figure in his earlier, more
feathery style. In the earlier version the woman
wears a less tailored costume with a frilled skirt,
lace collar and cuffs, and a hat. Cross-sections
of paint samples taken from this figure (p. 24)
provided an important tool for understanding
the successive stages of the painting [67]. In the
earlier phase of work, Renoir used exclusively
cobalt blue pigment, as he did in all his paintings
of the 1870s and early 1880s, while in the
later phase of work – comprising the upper
layers of the sample – he used only French
(synthetic) ultramarine. Both pigments would
have been easily available to him, so the change
undoubtedly reflects an aesthetic decision.

Cobalt blue was used for the intensely saturated blue seen in the figure group at right, while French ultramarine, mixed with other pigments, was used for the more muted, slate-grey tonality that pervades the remainder of the painting. Between the first campaign and the second Renoir also changed the yellow pigment he used. In the earlier phase of work he used zinc yellow (zinc potassium chromate), while in the later, Naples yellow (lead-tin-antimony yellow) was used. A new process for manufacturing genuine Naples yellow of much improved purity and strength of colour was introduced in 1878, leading to the increased popularity of this pigment in the late nineteenth century. The presence of one or the other of these blue or yellow pigments thus provided a marker for determining whether an aspect of the painting belonged to the artist's initial campaign or his later reworking. It became clear, for example, that the umbrellas were only introduced in the later phase of work as they were painted entirely in synthetic ultramarine.

At the close of the first stage of painting *The Umbrellas*, when he felt he could go no further, Renoir may have removed the canvas from the stretcher and rolled it for storage, which would account for the cracking now evident in the ground and paint layers. When he returned to the painting some five years later, he reduced its dimensions slightly. Areas of paint present on the turnover edges – where the canvas turns over the side of the wooden stretcher – at the left, top and bottom of the picture indicate that the canvas was cut down and mounted on a smaller stretcher, probably between the two stages of work. Interestingly, when scientists examined the paint cross-sections they found no evidence of varnish or dirt between the layers corresponding to the first and second phases of work: in fact the interfaces are unusually blended in parts. The most likely explanation is that Renoir washed down the painting with a solvent or cleaning agent before he started the second phase of painting. This may have slightly softened the paint in some areas, allowing it to fuse with the new layer above.

Why did Renoir abandon work on *The Umbrellas*, only to return to it five years later? Why did he completely rework some parts of the painting and others not at all, leaving a disjuncture between the two areas? We can only speculate. *The Umbrellas* is Renoir's last monumental painting of a contemporary urban subject, a theme absolutely central to the spirit of Impressionism, and it documents a critical turning point in his art. Coaxing solid, believable forms from the feathery and insubstantial Impressionist technique that he had mastered may have seemed an insurmountable challenge; but on the other hand the crisper, more angular shapes defining his style in 1886 may have seemed too severe for the light-hearted modernism of his subject. *The Umbrellas* is at once a farewell to Impressionism and a look forward to the more timeless and classical themes that Renoir preferred to address in the latter part of his career.

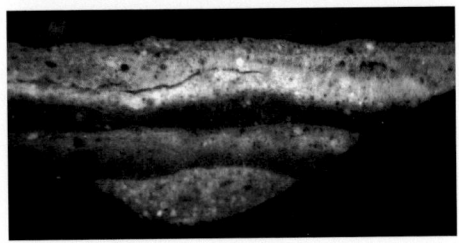

67. Pierre-Auguste Renoir (1841–1919), *The Umbrellas*, about 1881–6. Cross-section of a paint sample taken from the bodice of the woman at the left, revealing the original colour design below and the surface modification above. The principal pigments in the lower layers are cobalt blue, zinc yellow and red lake. A layer of the French ultramarine used in the later reworking of the composition is visible near the top of the upper layers.

CASE STUDY 11:
FORM AND FUNCTION

Dosso Dossi, *A Man embracing a Woman*, about 1524

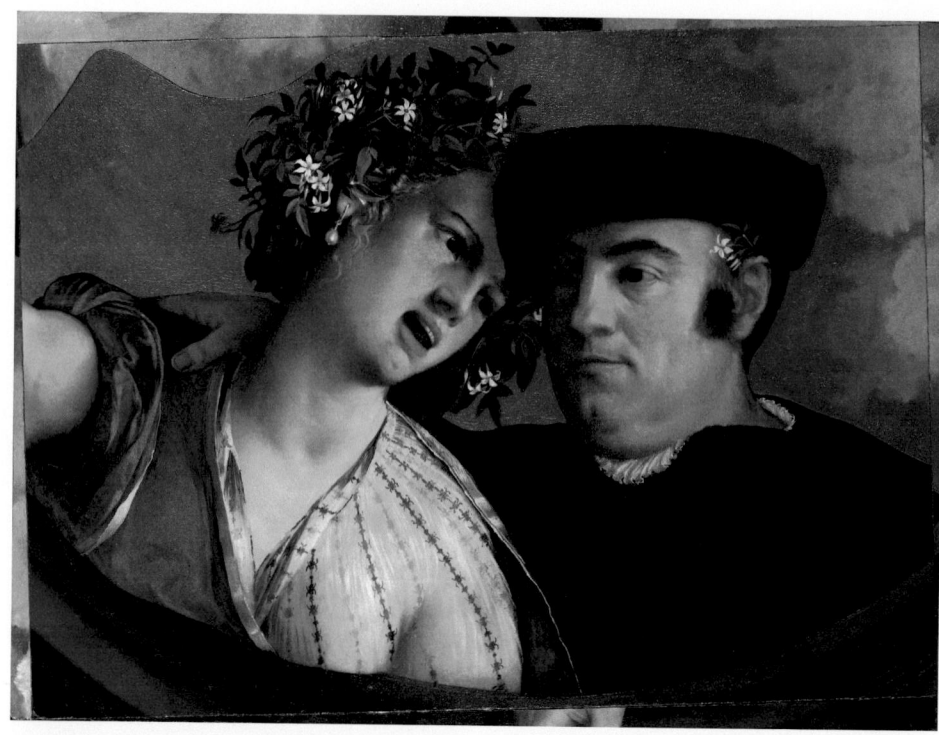

The subject of Dosso Dossi's *A Man embracing a Woman* is obscure. The current title is cautiously utilitarian, and for many years it was fancifully identified as a portrait of the poet Boccaccio and his mistress Fiametta. But even more curious is its peculiar physical structure. The two figures and most of the curved parapet before them are painted on a single, irregularly shaped piece of poplar with a pronounced diagonal grain, canted slightly anti-clockwise. The panel has been brought to a rectangular format through the addition of suitably shaped bits of wood, which were all cut from the same

painted panel. Obviously this striking image once had quite a different appearance.

In 1980 a detailed study was made of the painting's construction and technique. X-ray images [69] showed that the woman's headdress originally consisted not of flowers but of stiff tufts, and that the man had originally been bare-headed. By adding the hat, and making it overlap the woman's forehead, Dosso probably sought to make the man appear to be closer to the parapet edge. Cross-sections taken of paint samples (p. 23) revealed a complex layer structure, particularly in the background [70].

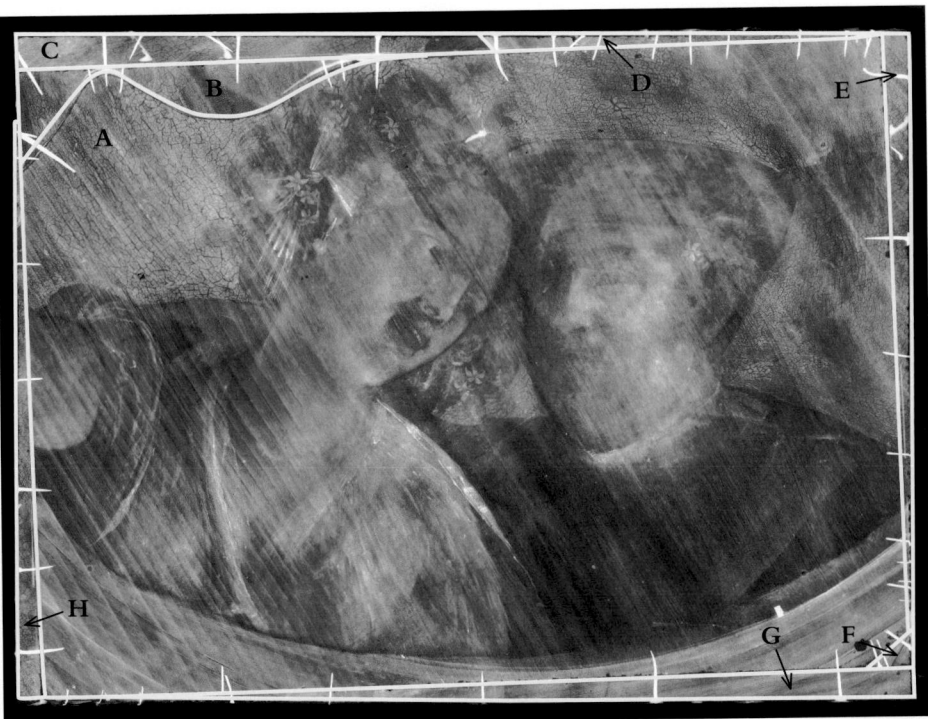

Over a dark grey underlayer are two layers
of brown paint, a thin discontinuous layer of
warm golden yellow and an unpigmented layer
that FTIR microscopy and GC–MS (pp. 26–8)
have identified as a rare survival of a sixteenth-
century varnish of resin from the sandarac tree.
Only after this varnish layer was the blue paint
of the background applied. This consists of an
underpaint of azurite (a cheaper blue pigment)
mixed with lead white, over which was applied
a layer of high quality (and extremely expensive)
natural ultramarine. These multiple layers
probably led to the wrinkling and cracking
that has affected the surface, especially in the
background areas.

Examining the painted surfaces and
orientation of the wood grain in the individual
fragments made it possible to reconstruct the
original context of *A Man embracing a Woman*.
It was conceived as part of a large circular
panel, or *tondo*; the near life-sized scale of
the figures and their proximity to the curved
parapet suggests that it might have been made
as a very specific type of decorative painting
[71]. A popular conceit in illusionistic ceiling
decorations was to represent figures as if leaning

over a parapet edge peering down into the room below. In 1524 Alfonso d'Este, Duke of Ferrara, commissioned Dosso to paint a *tondo* for the ceiling of the Camera del Poggiolo in Ferrara. Subsequent descriptions of this painting, coupled with existing knowledge of the National Gallery picture's history, made it possible to link the work with this important commission. Interestingly, in 1524 and again in 1526, Dosso received payments from d'Este specifically to reimburse him for the expensive ultramarine used in the *tondo*.

In 1608 Dosso's *tondo* was transferred from Ferrara to the Borghese collection in Rome. Deprived of its original context, the unusual circular format became a liability, and sometime after 1700 and before 1828 the painting was cut into sections – undoubtedly to make them more saleable. As it is now impossible to reconstitute Dosso's *tondo* for the Camera del Poggiolo from the surviving fragments, it was decided not to dismantle the current assemblage of *A Man embracing a Woman*. It remains as an extreme example of the alterations that paintings may undergo in the course of their history.

71. Reconstruction of the ceiling *tondo* from the Camera del Poggiolo, Ferrara, showing probable original positions of the identified surviving fragments of *A Man embracing a Woman*. The fragment at upper right, *Boy with a Basket of Flowers*, is in the Fondazione Roberto Longhi, Florence.

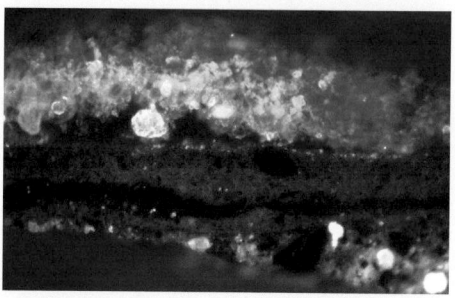

70. Cross-section of a paint sample taken from the blue background of *A Man embracing a Woman*. From bottom to top, the sample reveals a grey underlayer, two layers of brownish paint with a thin interlayer of unpigmented material, an unpigmented translucent layer (probably sandarac varnish), a layer of azurite and lead white, and a bright blue surface paint containing high-quality ultramarine.

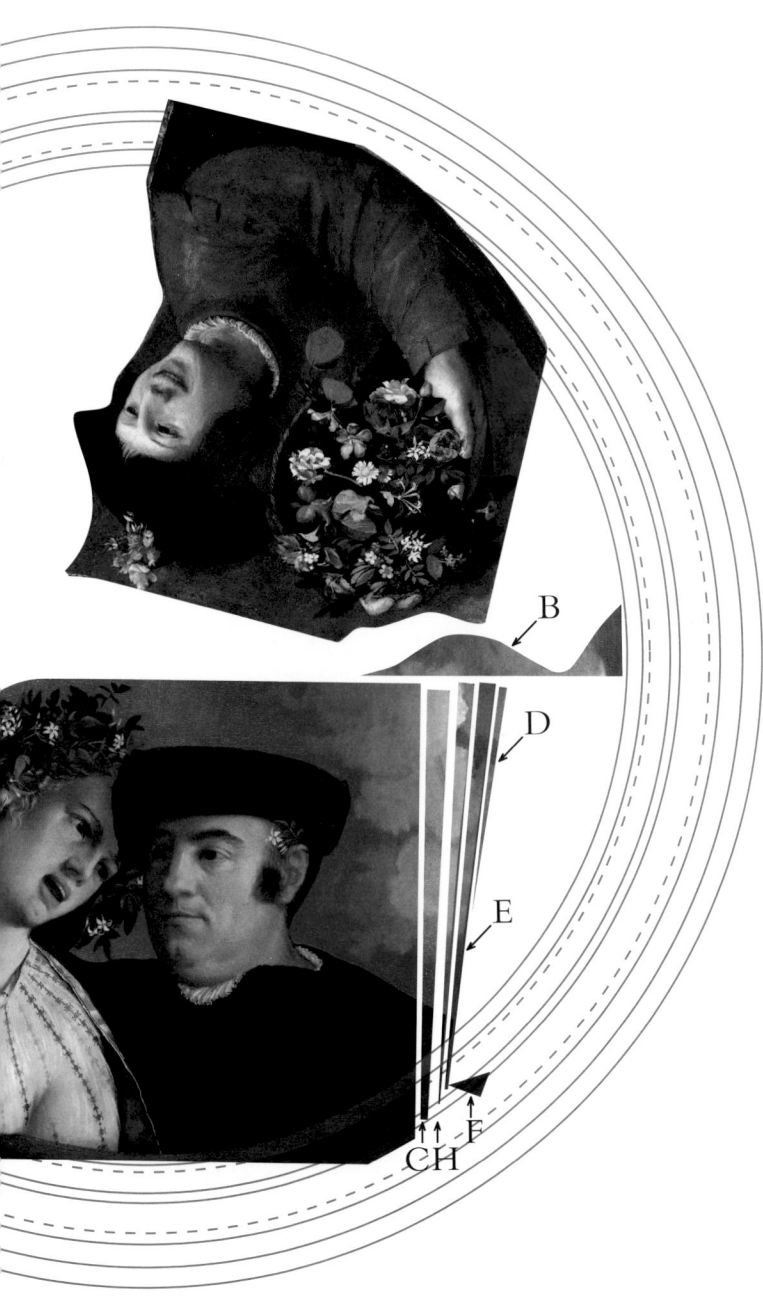

B

D

E

F

CH

CASE STUDY 12:
TIME, TASTE AND TRANSFORMATION I

Master of the Mornauer Portrait, *Portrait of Alexander Mornauer*, about 1464–88

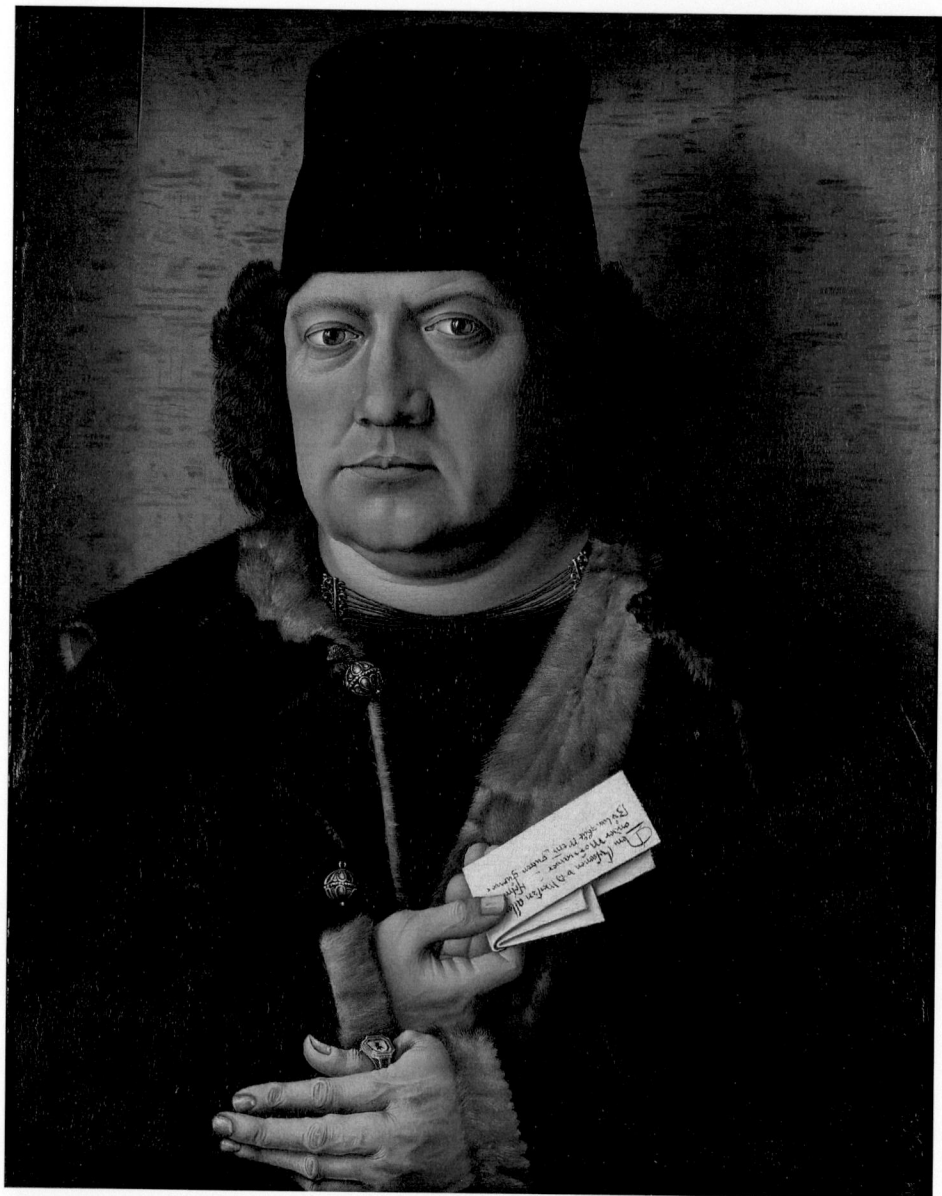

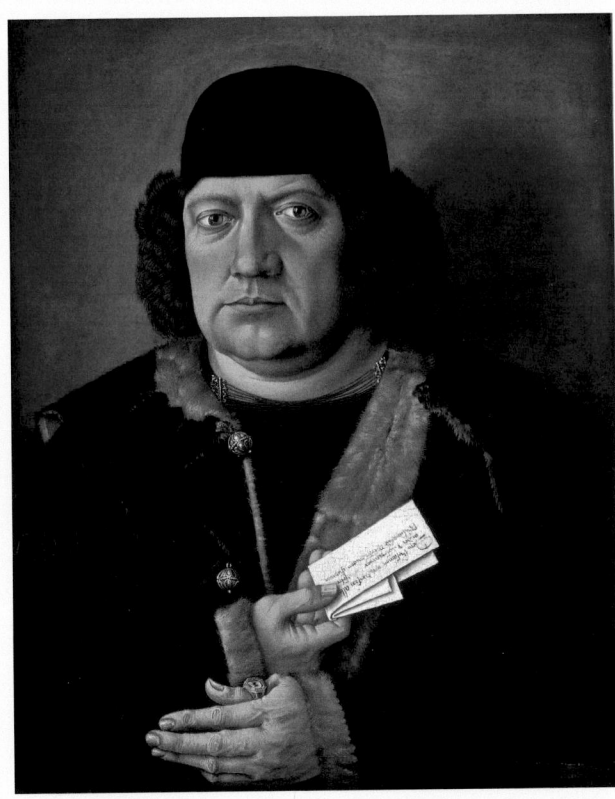

Opposite page: 72. Master of the Mornauer Portrait (probably active about 1460–1488), *Portrait of Alexander Mornauer*, probably about 1464–88, oil on wood, 45.2 x 38.7 cm.

Left: 73. *Portrait of Alexander Mornauer* before cleaning, showing the overpainted blue background and fitted cap.

The subject of this striking portrait is identified by name and occupation on the letter he holds, which reads (in translation): 'To the honourable and wise Alexander Mornauer, town clerk of Landshut, my good patron.' Mornauer held the post of town clerk in the Bavarian city of Landshut from 1464 until 1488. The seal ring he wears on his thumb depicts a moor's head, presumably a punning reference on his name.

When the painting was acquired by the National Gallery in 1990, the background was a deep blue and Mornauer's hat fitted closely to the crown of his head [73]. Neither reflected the artist's original intent. After the removal of an extremely discoloured varnish by National Gallery conservators, it became evident that both the texture and colour of the blue background paint were unusual for the fifteenth

century. Small samples of paint were taken to identify the original materials used. Examined in cross-section with EDX (p. 25, fig 74), the brilliant blue overpaint was found to contain Prussian blue – a pigment invented between 1704 and 1710, but not in widespread use until the 1720s. GC-MS showed the medium in the overpaint to be a heat-bodied poppyseed oil, an unlikely paint binder for a fifteenth-century picture, while the original paint was bound in linseed oil, a more typical medium for the period.

The blue overpaint was separated from the original paint layers by two layers of natural resin varnish, confirming that it had been applied some time after the original painting was made [75]. As it was clearly a later addition it could be safely removed, revealing

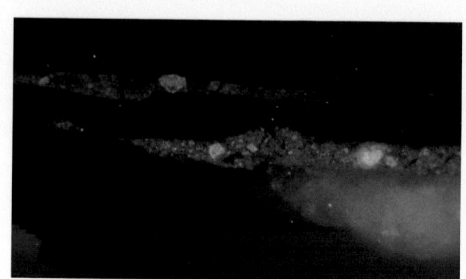

74. Master of the Mornauer Portrait (probably active about 1460–1488), *Portrait of Alexander Mornauer*, probably about 1464–88. Cross-section of paint sample taken from *Portrait of Alexander Mornauer* before the removal of bright blue overpaint from the background. The original light-brown paint is isolated from this later addition by a thick, translucent layer of discoloured varnish.

a background with a horizontally grained wood pattern – an effect seen in other German paintings of the period – and a taller hat that extends almost to the top of the panel. As the original background paint is in excellent condition, the blue overpaint must have been introduced for some reason other than to hide an area of damage. But when was this done, and why?

The history of the painting is not known before its acquisition by George Nugent-Temple-Grenville, 1st Marquess of Buckingham, between 1788 and 1797. At that time it was called a portrait of Martin Luther, by Hans Holbein the Younger, and both reproductions and written descriptions indicate the painting was then already in its overpainted state. The bold frontal pose of the figure in the *Portrait of Alexander Mornauer* is superficially reminiscent of portraits by Holbein painted a few decades later, so the vivid blue background may have been added, and the hat modified, to heighten the resemblance to his works. Certainly a portrait by a celebrated master of such a famous sitter would have held greater appeal for the eighteenth-century collector than a portrait by an anonymous artist of the town clerk of Landshut. The painting therefore appears to

have been modified between about 1720, when Prussian blue became widely available, and the last decade of the eighteenth century, when it entered the Buckingham collection. These changes were almost certainly implemented to pass it off as a work by Holbein, one of the most sought-after artists of the sixteenth century (case study 5).

The alterations to the background and hat were thus made later, but X-radiographs and infrared reflectograms (pp. 21, 22) also revealed changes made by the artist while he was painting [75]. The most significant of these was to Mornauer's left hand, which was first underdrawn and painted with the thumb pointing downwards and the fingers disappearing into the folds of his coat.

Other changes, albeit unintentional ones, have also affected the portrait's appearance since it was first created. Mornauer's hat and robe, painted with a mixture of mineral azurite and red lake, would originally have been a deep purple, but these have darkened and become brown over time. His underrobe was painted with vermilion and red lake pigment, glazed with pure red lake, then adjusted with the same purplish mixture used for the outer garment; this, too, must have darkened to some extent.

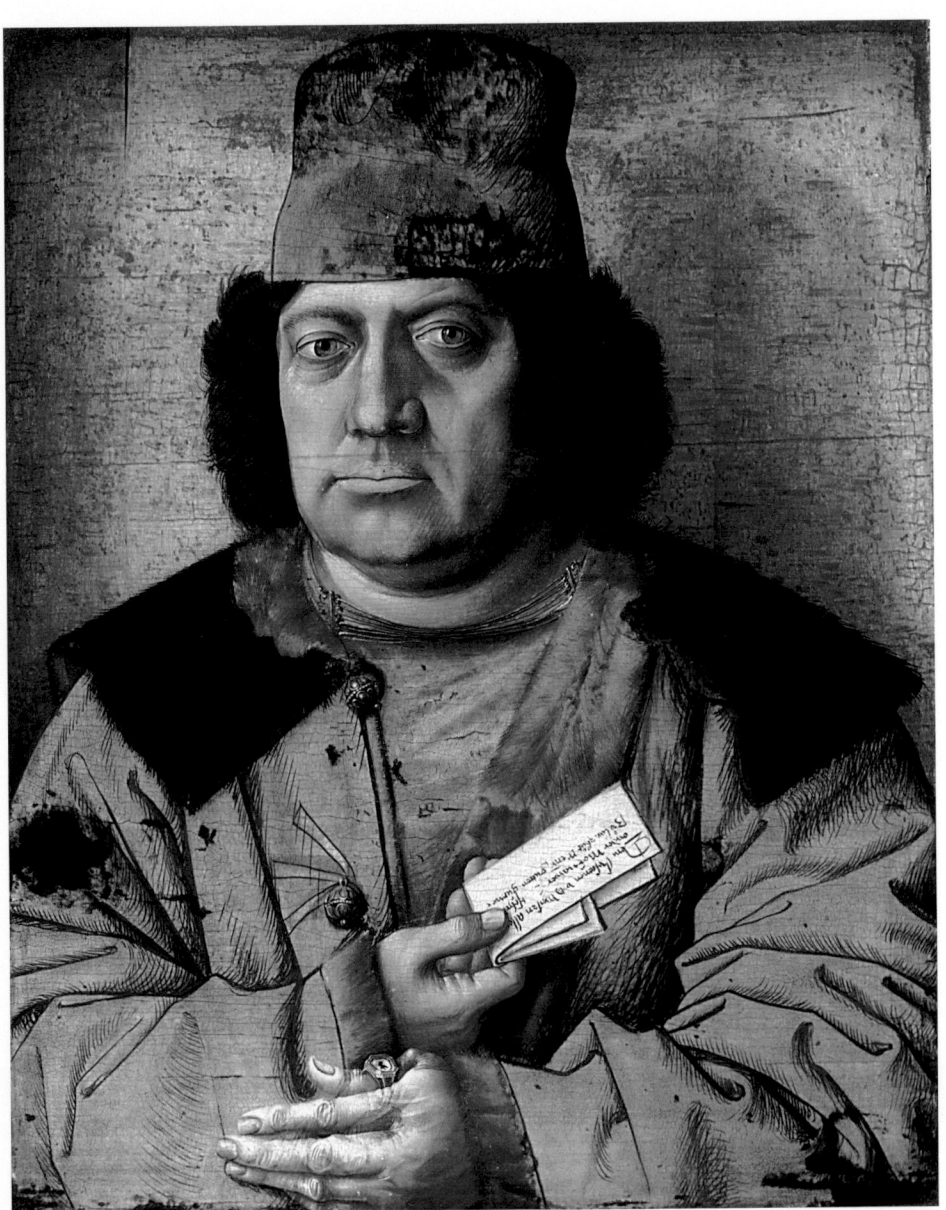

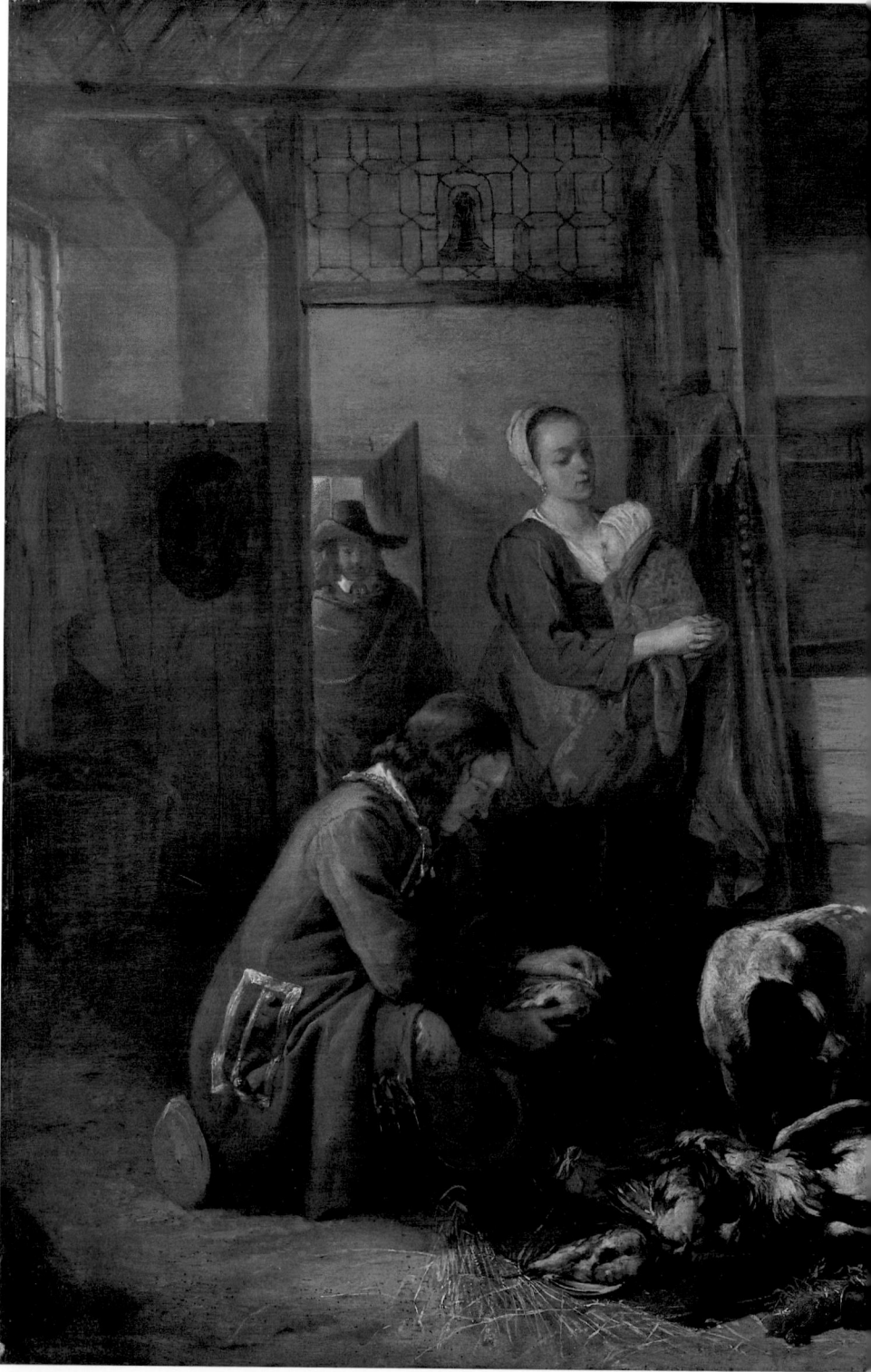

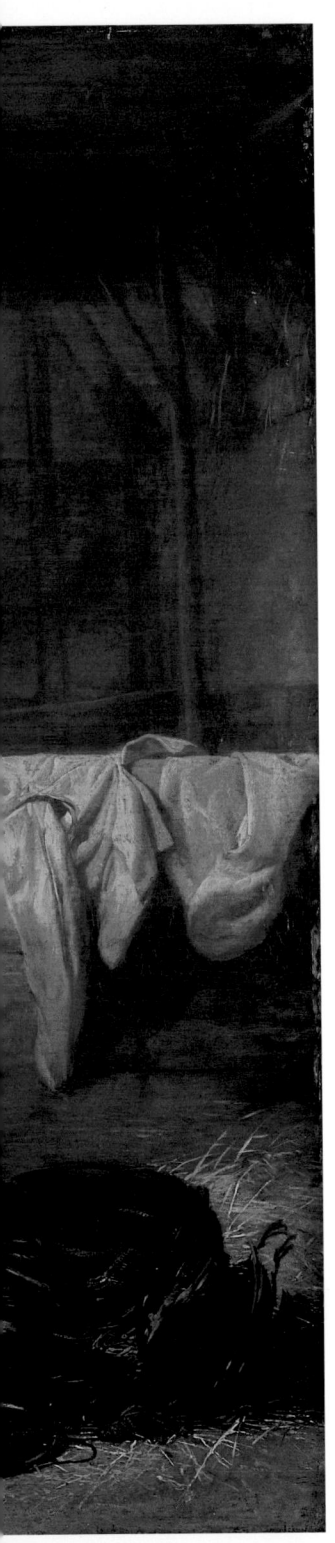

CASE STUDY 13:
TIME, TASTE AND TRANSFORMATION II

Pieter de Hooch, *A Man with Dead Birds, and other Figures, in a Stable*, about 1655

A Man with Dead Birds, and other Figures, in a Stable entered the National Gallery in 1924 as a rare example of de Hooch's early work. The humble setting and almost monochrome palette are entirely characteristic of works produced by the Delft painter around 1655. Nonetheless, the painting had been sold in 1900 as a work by Jan Baptist Weenix, the seventeenth-century Dutch painter of game and bird still lifes, and was later described as a collaborative work by Weenix and de Hooch. Although Weenix's involvement in the picture was rightly dismissed, the vacillating attribution reflects the stylistic discrepancy between the richly painted still life in the foreground and the remainder of the picture, which is more thinly painted (and rather worn), and limited in palette.

In 1971 X-ray and infrared photographs (pp. 21–3) were taken to determine if a connection could be made between the National Gallery picture and a remarkably similar painting by de Hooch that was then presumed to be lost. The catalogue of an

76. Pieter de Hooch (1629–1684), *A Man with Dead Birds, and other Figures, in a Stable*, about 1655, oil on oak, 53.5 x 49.7 cm.

77. X-radiograph of *A Man with Dead Birds, and other Figures, in a Stable* (detail).

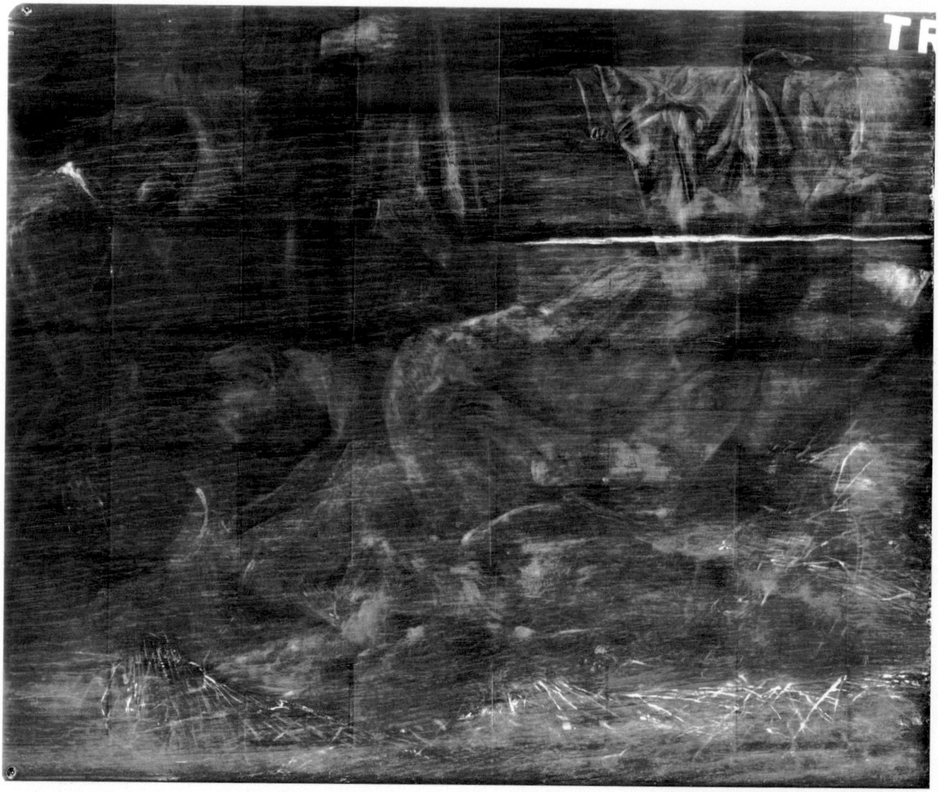

78. Thin cross-section of a paint sample taken from the greyish-blue plumage of the bird at lower right of *A Man with Dead Birds, and Other Figures, in a Stable*. The bottom two layers are original paint, the lower consisting of a synthetic copper blue pigment (probably blue verditer), lead white, smalt, earth pigments and some calcium carbonate, while the upper darker layer contains a copper blue pigment, carbon black and earth pigments. The blue-grey overpaint on top consists predominantly of ultramarine, Naples yellow, lead white, smalt, red earth and some calcium sulphate.

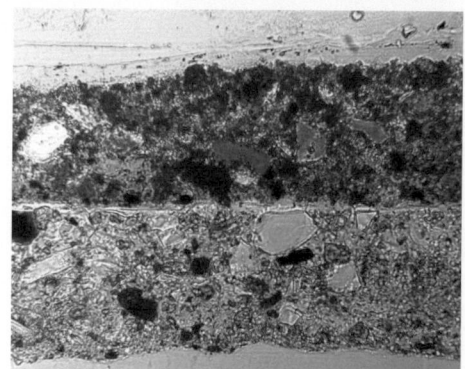

auction in 1825 described the latter as 'A stable interior, in the foreground lies a wounded man who is being bandaged by a surgeon...'.

The X-ray image proved these pictures [77] to be one and the same: the spaniel and dead birds had been painted over the figure of a reclining man, positioned with his head near the panel's right edge and his body laid almost parallel to the picture plane. His bent right leg was supported by the hands of the soldier now seen to be plucking feathers from a bird.

The figure was thus probably overpainted with the still life between 1825, when the painting was described as depicting a wounded man, and 1900, when it was sold in its present state. The buyer at the auction in 1825 was given as 'Regemorter': probably the Antwerp painter Ignatius Van Regemorter, who specialised in painting anecdotal scenes inspired by the lives of seventeenth-century Dutch artists. Both Ignatius and his father were also active as dealers, picture restorers and copyists – and evidently did not always act with absolute integrity. In 1797 it was noted: 'Regemortel [sic] of Antwerp is ... making Ruisdaels, Pynackers, Boths, etc. He is very busy. Before long we will probably see an assortment of all those great masters, whose names he is good at putting on his overpainted pictures. It is a pity, I think, that honest folk are duped by this.' The Van Regemorters seem to have altered some of the older paintings that passed through their hands to suit contemporary taste. De Hooch's choice of a rather sobering

subject – a wounded man – and the painting's generally worn condition may have prompted Van Regemorter to adapt the picture creatively when he acquired it in 1825.

In an effort to determine the age of the painting more precisely, in 2009 scientists took minute paint samples from a few key areas. Analysis of a cross-section of paint layers from a sample of the greyish-blue plumage of the bird at lower right confirmed the main components to be natural ultramarine, Naples yellow, lead white, smalt and red earth in the uppermost, or overpaint, layer [78]. Use of Naples yellow (lead-antimony yellow) replaced lead-tin yellow during the first quarter of the eighteenth century, then rose and fell in popularity until the latter part of the nineteenth century.

In contrast, a sample taken from an area of original paint was found to contain the lead-tin yellow commonly used by seventeenth-century Dutch painters, though still in use during the first quarter of the eighteenth century. In spite of the presence of Naples yellow, the combination of pigments present in the area of overpaint does not allow it to be dated more specifically within the known parameters (1825–1900). Nonetheless the materials identified in cross-section are consistent with evidence from the 1825 auction catalogue, making it clear that de Hooch's sombre *A Man with Dead Birds, and other Figures, in a Stable Interior* was made more 'saleable' by an unscrupulous painter-dealer during the nineteenth century.

CASE STUDY 14:
NEW APPRECIATION FOR THE ARTIST

Sandro Botticelli, *Saint Francis of Assisi with Angels*, about 1475–80

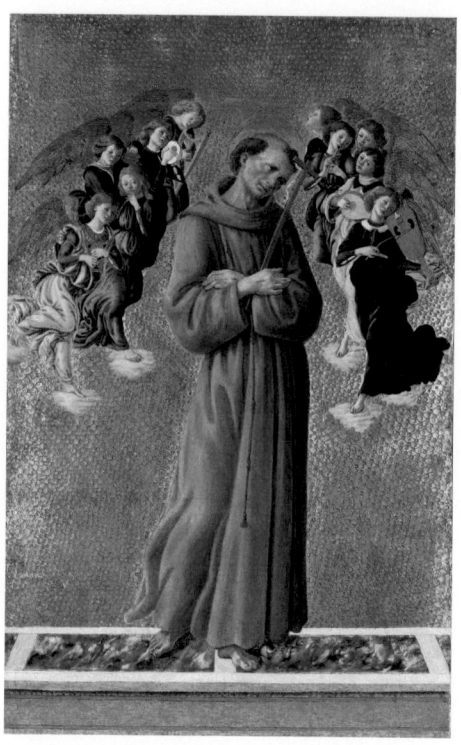

79. Sandro Botticelli (about 1445–1510),
Saint Francis of Assisi with Angels, about 1475–80,
tempera and oil on wood, 49.5 x 31.8 cm.

Clumsy restorations and a fixed conception of an artist's work can sometimes hamper appreciation of a painting's merit. In 1858 Charles Lock Eastlake acquired *Saint Francis of Assisi with Angels* for the National Gallery from the Costabili collection in Ferrara as a work by Botticelli's younger colleague and assistant, Filippino Lippi. At that time the painting bore an inscription along the simulated stone ledge in the lower foreground and a date of 1492. It was difficult to reconcile this relatively late date with the style of the work, however, particularly the use of a gilded background. Some scholars speculated that this was a deliberately retrospective element, influenced by the apocalyptic preachings of the Dominican zealot Fra Girolamo Savonarola in Florence in the 1490s.

When the *Saint Francis* was cleaned in 1940, the inscription along the front of the marble ledge at the base of the painting was discovered to be a later addition – indeed, the whole strip was found to have been repainted. Among the pigments identified in samples taken from this repainted area was Prussian blue, only discovered between 1704 and 1710. Lying on top of this blue overpaint, the inscription must therefore have been applied at a point after the first decade of the eighteenth century and before 1841, when it was first noted in a Costabili collection catalogue. Fragments of paint beneath the layer of later overpaint contained the blue pigment azurite and a small fragment of gold leaf. This suggested that the lettering added in the eighteenth or early nineteenth centuries may have been an attempt to reproduce an

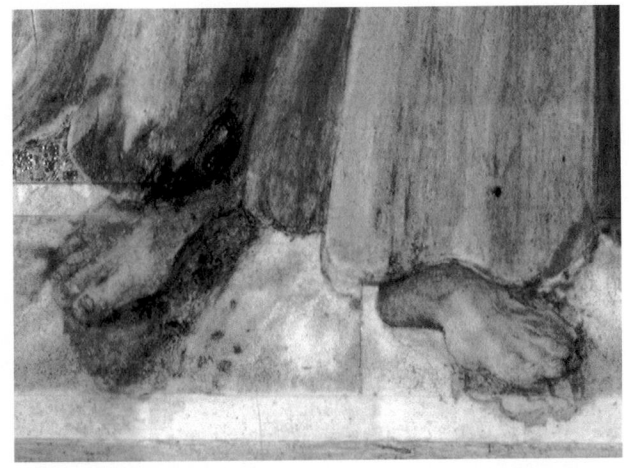

earlier inscription that had become worn, damaged or partly illegible.

With the removal of the false inscription the painting was no longer tied to a date of 1492, but a definite attribution of the work seemed no closer. Scholars had expressed doubt about the painting's traditional attribution to Filippino Lippi, but were unable to agree on who might have painted it. Various names were proposed; intriguingly, the renowned connoisseur Bernard Berenson considered the painting to be a copy of a lost early work by Botticelli. By the mid-twentieth century *Saint Francis* had been classified as by a follower of Botticelli, painted under the influence of the master's early style, and was relegated to the National Gallery's reserve collection.

The *Saint Francis* was cleaned and restored in 2002, in connection with the Gallery's ongoing programme of re-cataloguing the collection. Freed of old, unsympathetic retouchings it was revealed to be of much higher quality than had previously been appreciated, and was recognised as an authentic early work by Botticelli. An infrared reflectogram (p. 23) revealed changes made to the position of Saint Francis's left foot; additional changes to the right foot are visible with the naked eye. Such reworkings indicate that this is an original work and not a copy after

an existing model [80]. The angels' broad, heart-shaped faces are characteristic of Botticelli's paintings from the early 1470s, while the sinewy and emotionally charged figure of the saint has its closest parallels in works from the latter part of the decade. Decorative, two-dimensional gilded backgrounds, though largely outmoded by the 1490s, were not unknown in Florentine painting of the 1470s, and Botticelli may have incorporated one here in response to a patron's specific requirement. Although the figures are primarily painted using an egg tempera medium, Botticelli applied thin, oil-based glazes of colour over the gold to produce a shimmering, translucent effect on the angels' wings. Most of this delicate paint has now worn away, but remnants can be detected in the incisions outlining the feathers [81].

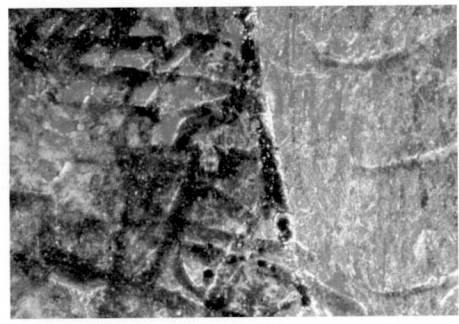

CASE STUDY 15:
RECOGNISING THE ORIGINAL I

Caspar David Friedrich, *Winter Landscape*, probably 1811

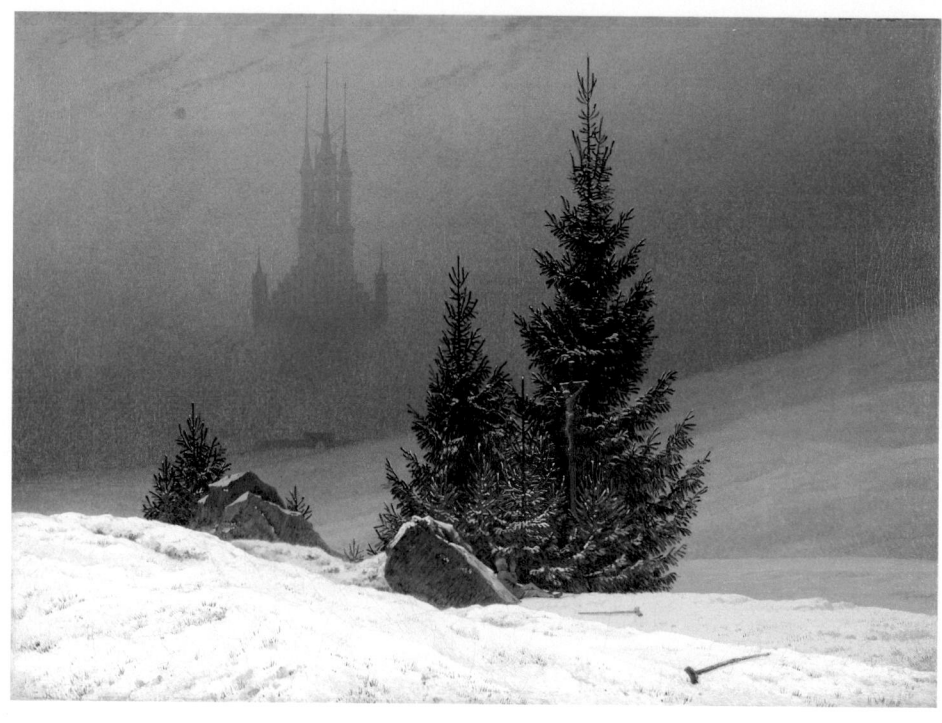

82.
Caspar David Friedrich (1774–1840),
Winter Landscape, probably 1811, oil on canvas,
32.5 x 45 cm.

Friedrich's *Winter Landscape* was discovered in a private collection in Paris in 1982, and was acquired by the National Gallery five years later. The painting appeared identical in nearly every respect to a version that had been in the Museum für Kunst und Kulturgeschichte in Dortmund since 1940 [83]. Yet only one version of the composition was recorded in nineteenth-century documents, so which painting was the original?

Although the paintings appear at first to be near identical, there are details in the London painting which do not appear in the Dortmund picture. The most noticeable are the

83. Caspar David Friedrich (1774–1840), *Winter Landscape with a Church*, probably 1811 or later, oil on canvas, 33 x 45 cm. Museum für Kunst und Kulturgeschichte, Dortmund.

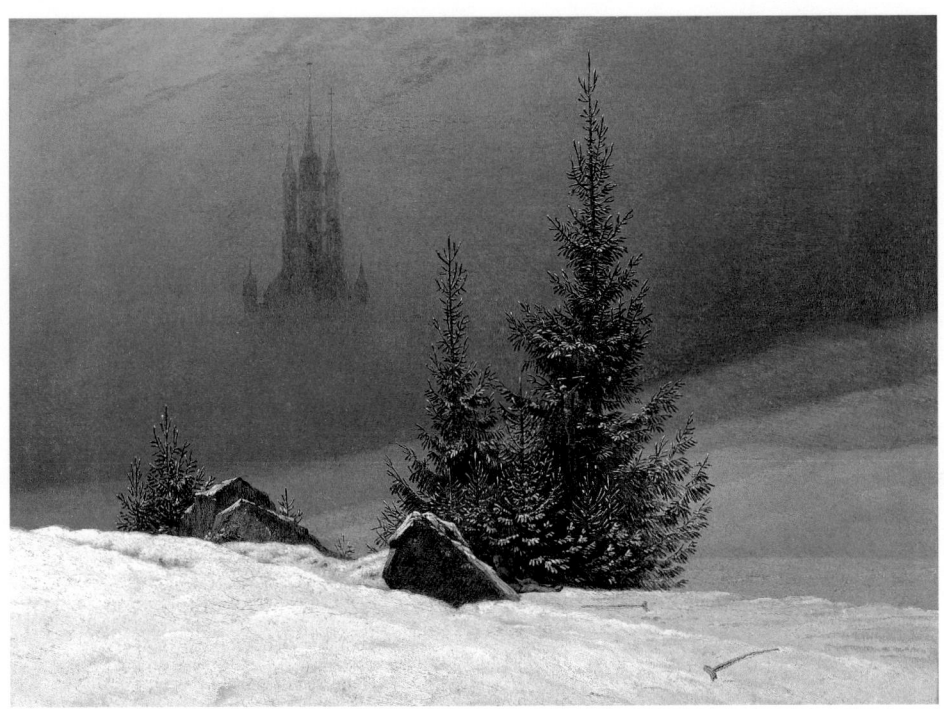

gateway in front of the church and the blades of grass poking through the melting snow in the foreground. While the Dortmund version is rendered with a broad, spontaneous touch, the precise, controlled handling of the London picture in fact relates more closely to Friedrich's early style of painting. Friedrich began his career as a draughtsman, and when he turned to oil painting in 1807 he simply adapted his usual methods to the new medium. He applied the oil paint in thin, transparent washes over a delicate underdrawing, and the works he produced resembled coloured drawings more than paintings. He used a range of marks and

patterns, such as short, hatched strokes, stippling (paint applied in tiny points or dots) and a selective use of thickly textured paint, or impasto, to convey the surfaces and forms of nature [84, 85].

Friedrich took similar pains with the pigments he used in the *Winter Landscape*. Much of the scene is painted using just a few pigments – lead white, red earth and different grades of smalt, the blue glass pigment – suggesting that a subtle gradation of tones, rather than colouristic variety, was of primary importance in creating this evocative scene. The use of smalt is particularly interesting. Although synthetic blue

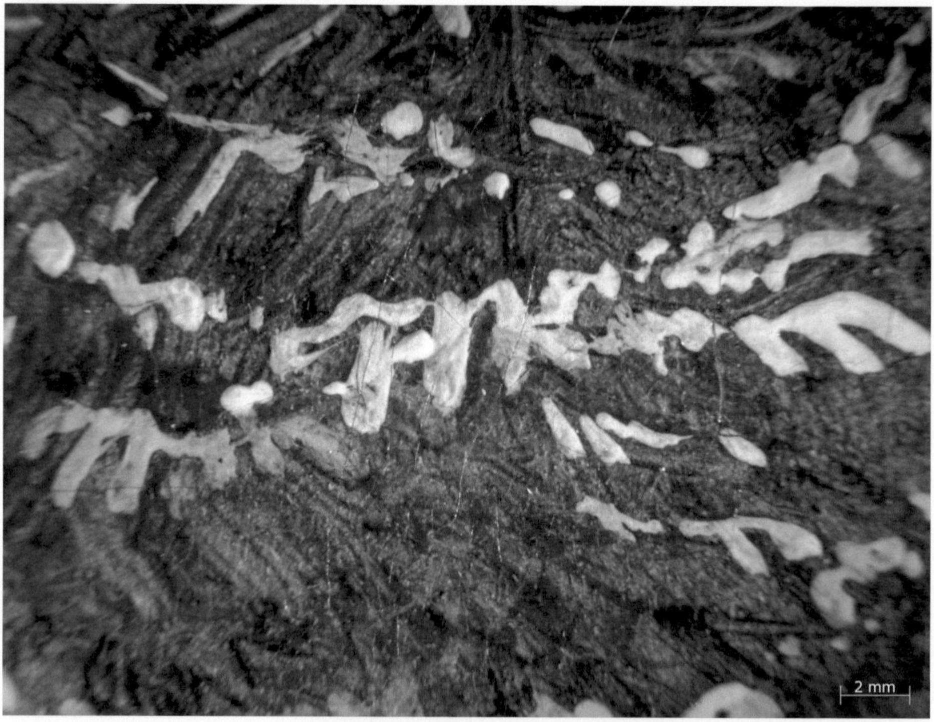

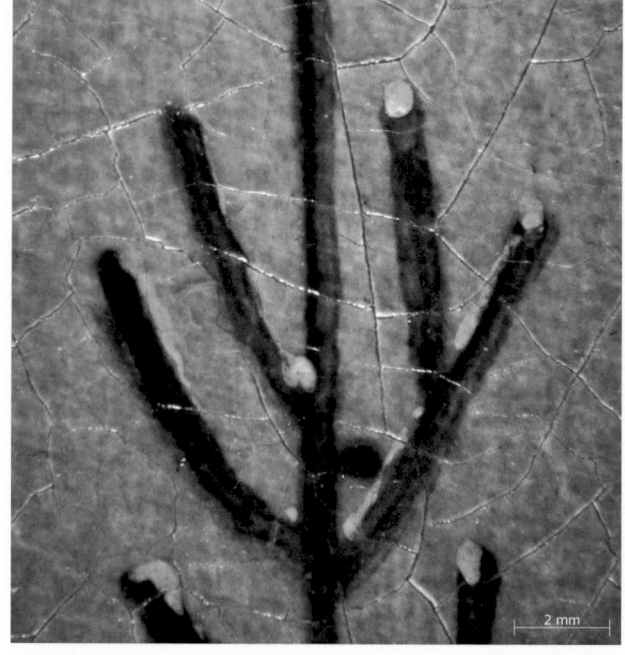

Above and right: 84 and 85.
Photomicrophotographs of
Winter Landscape, showing
varied textures of paint
application.

86. Detail of the infrared reflectogram of
Winter Landscape showing the extensive
underdrawing.

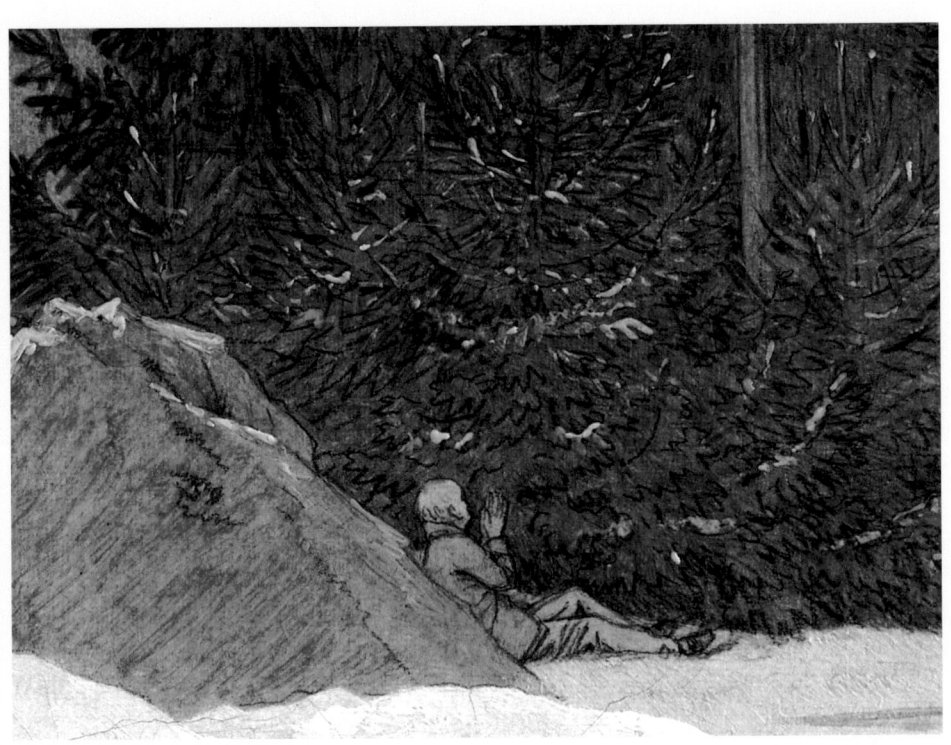

pigments such as cobalt and Prussian blue were popular and readily available, Friedrich chose the more traditional smalt for its translucent quality. He applied the paint in delicate stippled strokes that scatter the light, recreating the dissolving textures of a vaporous landscape.

Recent improvements in infrared imaging (pp. 22–3) have allowed a better understanding of the underdrawing of the *Winter Landscape* [86]. A slightly freer preliminary sketch – which appears paler in the infrared reflectogram – was reinforced with a stronger line marking the final placement of details. Both were executed in a liquid medium, probably with a brush. The basic structure of the church was marked out in the underdrawing with thin ruled lines. The church was painted in grey with details crisply drawn in black, then 'veiled' by the misty colours of the sky paint.

Although extensive underdrawing is a characteristic feature of Friedrich's paintings, none is visible in an infrared photograph of the Dortmund painting. This distinctly separates that work from other paintings by Friedrich that have been studied by infrared imaging. The Dortmund *Winter Landscape* is probably a replica by Friedrich, or possibly by a pupil or imitator. Its close similarity to the London painting suggests that it may have been made while the London painting was still in Friedrich's studio.

CASE STUDY 16:
RECOGNISING THE ORIGINAL II

Raphael, *Madonna of the Pinks ('La Madonna dei Garofani')*, about 1506–7

The sweet innocence of this gem-like depiction of a youthful Madonna enjoying a playful moment with her infant son gives no sign of the painting's turbulent critical history. Raphael painted the *Madonna of the Pinks* in 1506 or 1507, shortly before he left Florence for Rome. To judge from the dozens of surviving early copies and prints made of the composition, the painting was both famous and highly esteemed throughout the sixteenth and seventeenth centuries. It was first published as by Raphael in 1829, while in the collection of Pietro and Vincenzo Camuccini in Rome. Pietro Camuccini was a copyist, picture restorer and dealer, and his brother Vincenzo a leading neo-classical painter. In 1855 the painting was purchased, together with the rest of the Camuccini collection, by the 4th Duke of Northumberland. In the course of the nineteenth century, however, the picture's reputation was tarnished by the negative opinions of scholars, including Johann David Passavant, the great early authority on Raphael, who declared it merely the best of many copies after a lost original. Dismissed as a copy, the painting hung in a corridor, all but forgotten, for nearly a century. In 1991 the *Madonna of the Pinks* was 'rediscovered' by a National Gallery curator on a visit to Alnwick Castle, the home of the Dukes of Northumberland. After intensive technical and art historical research, this tiny painting was once again championed as the original by Raphael. With the aid of a generous public appeal and support from the Heritage Lottery Fund, the National Gallery acquired the painting in 2004.

The reinstatement of a painting such as the *Madonna of the Pinks* as an original work of art can be an intricate and complex process, usually involving the gradual accumulation of many small but significant pieces of evidence. When the painting was cleaned in 1991, it was found to have survived in exceptionally fine state. In style and technique it is absolutely characteristic of Raphael at this stage in his career, executed with a delicacy of touch and a great assuredness in the handling of the paint. The unusual attention to detail and exquisite finish are also seen in other small-scale paintings by Raphael. Scientific examination and analysis provided conclusive support for the visual assessment of the painting's quality and authenticity.

Microscopic examination identified the wood panel support as yew. It was prepared with a gesso ground, thinly coated with an off-white, oil-based *imprimitura*. Infrared reflectography revealed a detailed underdrawing made over the *imprimitura* in metalpoint [88, see p. 7], using a stylus made from an alloy of lead and tin, identified by EDX microanalysis (p. 23). Identical materials were used for the underdrawing in Raphael's slightly later *Garvagh Madonna*, also in the National Gallery. The underdrawing for the *Madonna of the Pinks* was done freehand, without the aid of a cartoon, and with considerable verve and variety. The mix of long, sweeping curves to define the larger forms of the body, rapid loops to indicate smaller forms and fine hatching to indicate shadows is entirely characteristic of Raphael and similar to his independent sketches on paper. For the most part Raphael followed

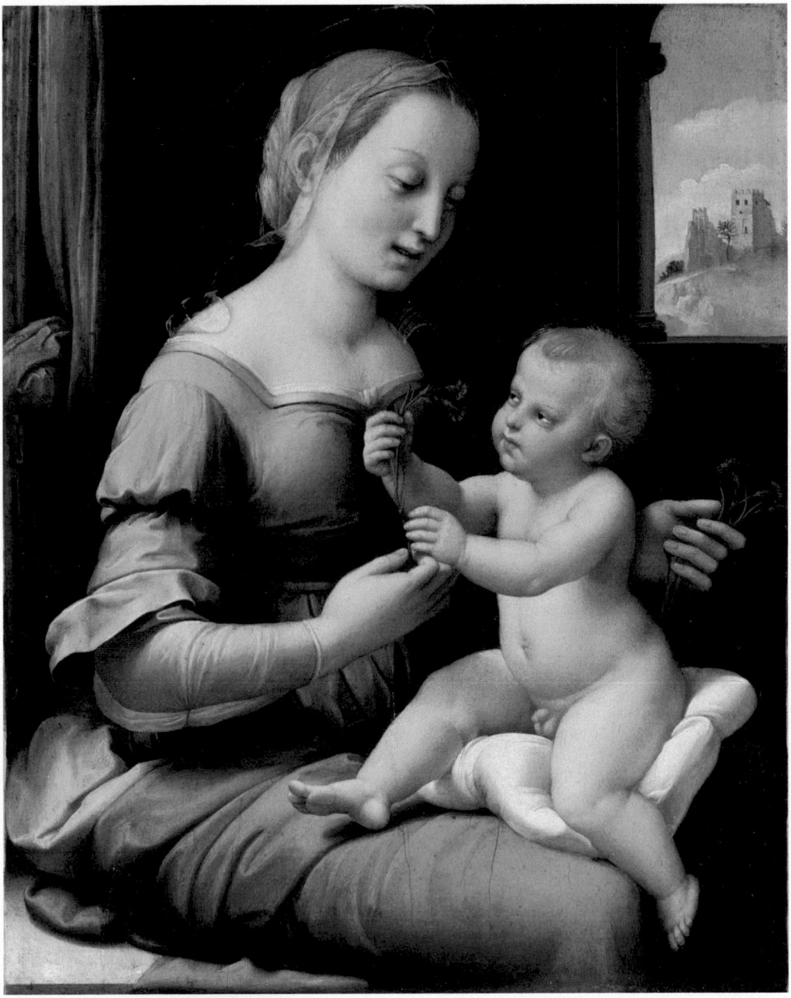

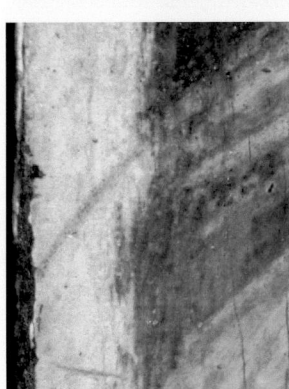

Above: 87. Raphael (1483–1520), *Madonna of the Pinks ('La Madonna dei Garofani')*, about 1506–7, oil on yew, 27.9 x 22.4 cm.

Left: 88. Photomicrograph of the knot in the curtain at the left edge of *Madonna of the Pinks* showing a stroke of the metalpoint underdrawing over the *imprimitura*.

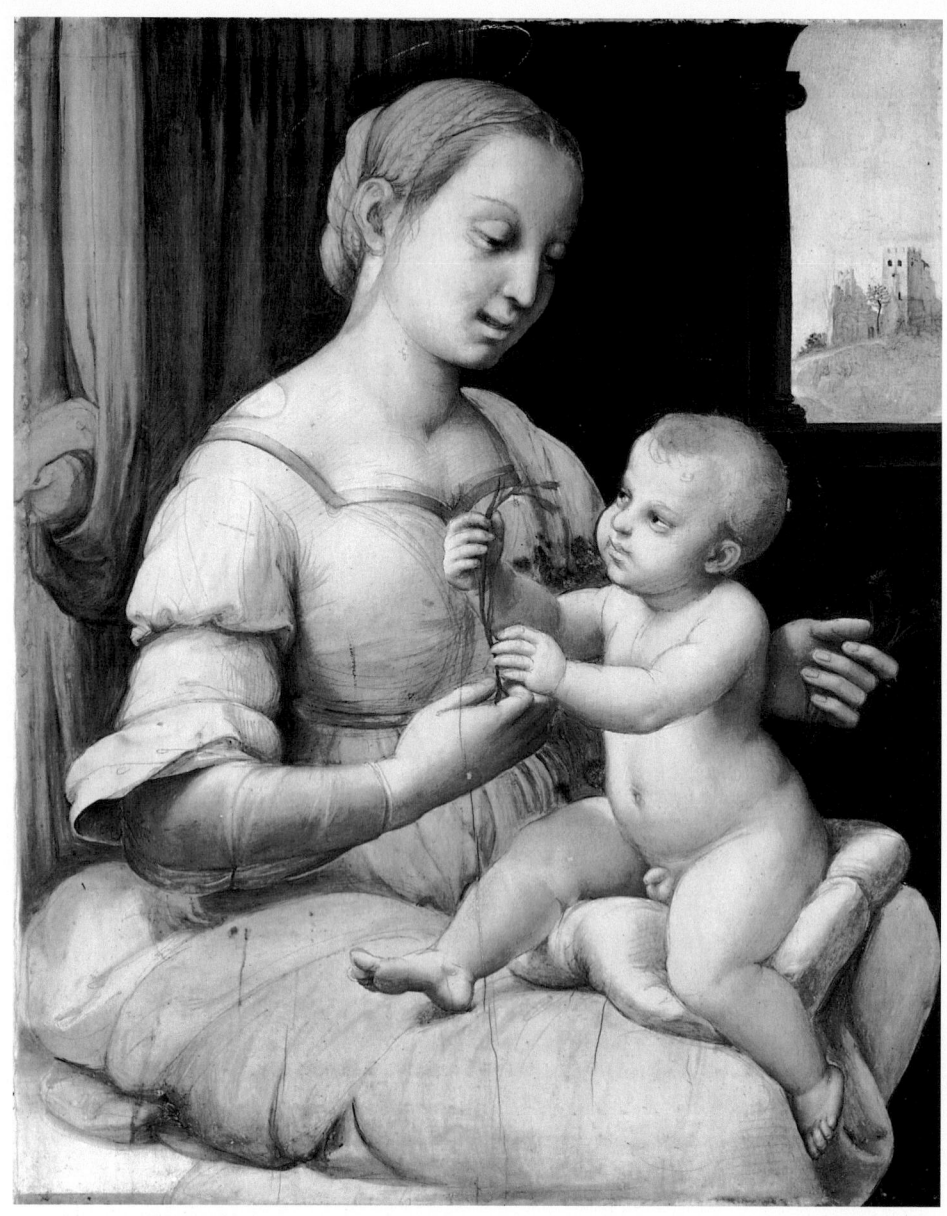

89. The underdrawing revealed in the
infrared reflectogram of *Madonna of
the Pinks* is varied and assured, similar
to Raphael's sketches on paper.

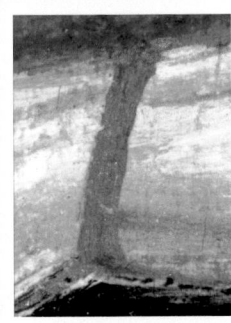
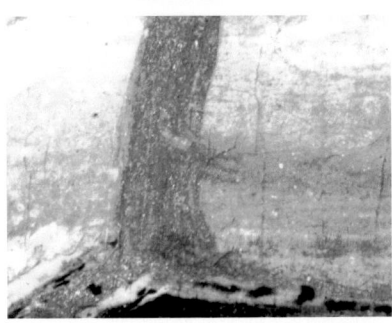

the principal outlines of the underdrawing closely as he painted, but some areas, such as the detail of the Virgin's bodice, were not fully resolved in the underdrawing, while in the landscape view at right the ruin, trees, and contour of the hill were drawn in different positions. The freedom and skill of the under-drawing, coupled with the evidence of changes made between the underdrawing and the finished painting, make it virtually impossible that this painting could be the work of a copyist.

The near-perfect condition of the paint surface meant that only a very limited number of samples could be taken, and then only from the extreme edge of the painted area. Fortunately the panel was small enough to permit direct examination at high magnification on the stage of a research microscope (p. 11) to help identify the pigments used. One significant finding was that both the blue of the Virgin's mantle and the sky at upper right were painted using natural ultramarine (lapis lazuli). In the sky the pigment is mixed with white; in the Virgin's blue drapery the ultramarine is painted over a greenish-blue underlayer containing mineral azurite, a less expensive blue pigment. The presence of both azurite and ultramarine in the same painting is entirely characteristic of sixteenth-century practice.

An unusual dark grey pigment with a distinctive sparkling metallic lustre was observed in the Virgin's belt, the shaded parts of her chemise sleeve and the ties on her sleeve [90, 91]. A pigment with similar microscopic appearance occurs in Raphael's *Ansidei Madonna*, also in the National Gallery, where it has been identified by EDX and XRD (pp. 23, 26) as powdered metallic bismuth, a chemical element. The same pigment, which is rarely found in paintings and seems to be restricted to those from the early sixteenth century, may well have been used in *Madonna of the Pinks*, but its presence cannot be confirmed as no physical sample could be taken from this perfectly preserved area. Although Raphael's palette is largely consistent with sixteenth-century practice, surprisingly it is the composition of the off-white *imprimitura* that is most telling. In addition to lead white and a little lead-tin yellow, it contains powdered glass of a particular type common in Italy at the time. This distinctive mixture is found in the *imprimitura* of many of Raphael's paintings.

The technical examination and analysis of the Gallery's *Madonna of the Pinks* confirm the visual assessment of the painting. Together they provide every indication that this finely wrought panel is indeed Raphael's original painting. The precise identification of techniques and materials, both generally consistent with early sixteenth-century paintings and specifically characteristic of Raphael, could not have been achieved without modern methods of scientific investigation and analysis. Hidden beneath the surface of the painting, these features would certainly not have been known to a later copyist.

GLOSSARY

Chromatography:
A method of separating mixtures in paint samples, enabling organic materials to be identified. The most common types of chromatography are **gas chromatography (GC-MS)** and **high performance liquid chromatography (HPLC)**. The sample's molecular components separate and are often analysed in a **mass spectrometer (MS)**.

Connoisseur:
A connoisseur is an expert, knowledgeable about a wide range of art and able to recognise characteristics of individual or regional styles.

Connoisseurship:
A stylistic attribution of a painting, usually made in conjunction with technical or historical research.

Craquelure:
The term used to described a network pattern of cracks that develops across the surface of a picture as the paint layers age and shrink.

Dendrochronology:
The widths of tree-rings in a wood panel are measured and analysed against a master chronology. To establish a date for a panel, allowances must be made for outer rings that have been trimmed, and for the time needed to season the wood before it was used for a painting. Dendrochronology can be used to date panels made from oak, but cannot be used for poplar because its growth is too erratic.

Energy dispersive X-ray spectrometer (EDX):
Used in conjunction with a **scanning electron microscope**, EDX works on the principle that the electron beam which scans the sample generates small amounts of X-rays, which are characteristic of the various elements that produce them. EDX is used to determine the elemental composition of a particle or layer within a paint cross-section.

Impasto:
A term used to describe highly textured paint that often bears visible brush or palette knife marks.

Infrared radiation (IR):
The portion of the electromagnetic spectrum that is found just beyond visible light.

Infrared reflectography (IRR) and Infrared photography:
Imaging methods used to 'see through' paint layers that are opaque to the human eye.
Infrared radiation (IR) passes through the paint until either it reaches something that absorbs it or it is reflected back to the camera. Carbon black is highly absorbing, so if an artist has begun a painting by drawing the design in black on a white ground, an infrared image can often show this **underdrawing**.
Infrared photography uses special film to record images. However, the narrow range of wavelengths used in infrared photography limits the pigments that it is possible to penetrate.
Infrared reflectography is capable of recording a wider range of wavelengths, allowing for more even penetration of different colours.

Mass spectrometer:
An analytical technique for the determination of the elemental composition and chemical structure of a molecule. The mass spectrometer ionises compounds to generate charged molecules or molecule fragments and measures their mass-to-charge ratios. It is often used in conjunction with **gas chromatography (GC-MS)** or **high performance liquid chromatography (HPLC)** to identify the separated components from organic materials.

Micron:
A unit of measurement. One micron is one thousandth of a millimetre, or one thousand nanometers.

Pentimento:
This term, Italian in origin, is used for a change made by the artist during the process of painting. Although these **pentimenti** (plural) are usually hidden, they can become visible if the subsequent paint layers have become more transparent with time.

Polarised light microscopy:
The investigation of the structure of pigment particles of a paint sample through a microscope equipped with a polarising light filter. Thin cross-sections or groups of particles may be examined in this way.

Raking light:
This describes the act of illuminating pictures at an oblique angle to reveal surface texture in greater contrast.

Raman microscopy:
A technique using a low-powered laser beam to identify the molecular structure of pigments. Under the laser beam, each substance in the sample scatters a characteristic combination of wavelengths

(known as its Raman spectrum). Raman microscopy is particularly useful for identifying the components of pigment mixtures.

Scanning electron microscope (SEM):
This microscope scans the surface of a sample with a beam of electrons, forming a detailed image of its topography and structure at a magnification of up to 100,000×. The results are analysed in an **energy-dispersive X-ray spectrometer (EDX)**.

Ultraviolet light:
A form of electromagnetic radiation with a wavelength shorter than that of visible light, but longer than X-rays. The sun emits ultraviolet radiation, so natural daylight has a UV component. Prolonged exposure to light from this part of the electromagnetic spectrum can damage many of the materials used in paintings, including the pigments and dyes, leading to problems such as discoloration, fading or cracking.

Underdrawing:
The preliminary drawing of a composition on a primed support, which is then painted over.

UV fluorescence microscopy:
The microscopic study of cross-sections under UV light, which causes some substances to fluoresce, giving off visible light. This reveals different colours which are characteristic of particular materials, such as pigments or varnishes.

X-radiograph:
A type of image made by placing sensitive film on the surface of the painting, and transmitting X-rays through the painting from the other side. Painting materials are mostly transparent to X-rays, but denser materials, such as lead-containing pigments or iron tacks, absorb the X-rays and appear light in the X-radiograph. These images are useful for revealing losses and changes to a painting that may have occurred during its history. X-radiographs can be difficult to interpret because the image shows all of the layers of the work superimposed.

X-ray diffraction (XRD):
A method of particle examination which is employed to identify crystalline pigments by analysis of their structure.

X-ray fluorescence (XRF):
A non-invasive technique which uses a focused beam of X-rays to identify the elements present in a sample area of painting.

FIND OUT MORE

More in-depth descriptions of the key methods of scientific examination and analysis can be found in: D. Pinna, M. Galeotti and R. Mazzeo (eds), *Scientific Examination for the Investigation of Paintings. A Handbook for Conservator-restorers*, Florence 2009.

In addition, many books on the conservation and restoration of paintings also address methods of, and approaches to, scientific examination and technical analysis. A particularly useful handbook is A. Kirsh and R.S. Levinson, *Seeing through Paintings: Physical Examination in Art Historical Studies*, New Haven and London 2000.

Detailed information on the pigments used in painting can be found in the series, *Artists' pigments: a handbook of their history and characteristics*, 4 vols, Cambridge, New York and Washington 1986-2007.

The following publications discuss various aspects of the scientific analysis of materials and techniques used in paintings in the National Gallery Collection:

D. Bomford, J. Dunkerton, D. Gordon and A. Roy, *Art in the Making: Italian Painting before 1400*, London 1989.

D. Bomford, J. Kirby, J. Leighton and A. Roy, *Art in the Making: Impressionism*, London 1990.

D. Bomford, ed., *Art in the Making: Underdrawings in Renaissance Paintings*, London 2002.

D. Bomford, S. Herring, J. Kirby, C. Riopelle and A. Roy, *Art in the Making: Degas*, London 2004.

D. Bomford, J. Kirby, A. Roy, A. Rüger and R. White, *Art in the Making: Rembrandt*, London 2006.

J. Dunkerton, S. Foister, D. Gordon and N. Penny, *Giotto to Dürer: Early Renaissance Painting in The National Gallery*, London and New Haven 1991.

J. Dunkerton, S. Foister and N. Penny, *Dürer to Veronese: Sixteenth-Century Painting in The National Gallery*, London and New Haven 1999.

S. Foister, A. Roy and M. Wyld, *Making and Meaning: Holbein's Ambassadors*, London 1997.

D. Gordon, *Making and Meaning: The Wilton Diptych*, London 1993.

Articles on the technical examination of paintings in the National Gallery Collection, as well as more wide-ranging studies of artists' materials and techniques, are published annually in the *National Gallery Technical Bulletin*. In addition, technical analysis of individual paintings forms an integral component of the National Gallery's ongoing series of schools catalogues.

DIAGRAM
CROSS-SECTION OF A
PAINTING

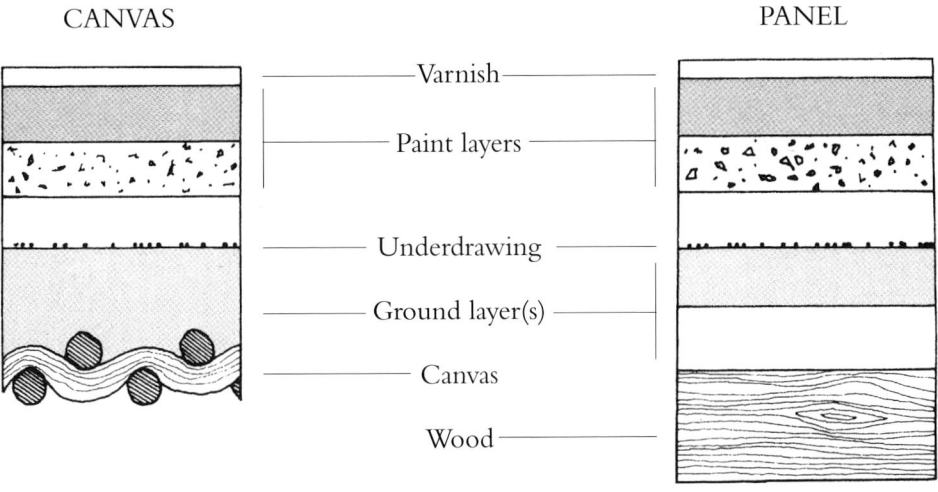

CANVAS

PANEL

Varnish

Paint layers

Underdrawing

Ground layer(s)

Canvas

Wood

ACKNOWLEDGEMENTS

Like a detailed technical investigation of a painting, this book is the product of collaborative research and collegial interaction between curators, scientists, conservators and archivists at the National Gallery. The willingness of colleagues to share their time and expertise has greatly enriched both the content of the book and the experience of preparing it. For their advice and valuable contributions to the text, I would especially like to thank Rachel Billinge, Lorne Campbell, Dawson Carr, Alan Crookham, Jill Dunkerton, Susan Foister, Sarah Herring, Helen Howard, Antonio Mazzotta, Scott Nethersole, Caroline New, David Peggie, Nicholas Penny, Carol Plazzotta, Chris Riopelle, Anne Robbins, Ashok Roy, Marika Spring, Luke Syson and Humphrey Wine.

OTHER TITLES IN THE *CLOSER LOOK* SERIES

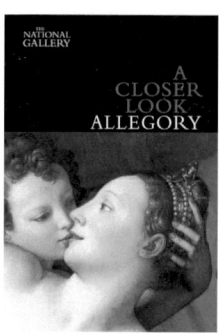

Allegory
Erika Langmuir
ISBN 978 1 85709 485 5

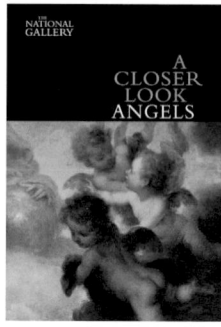

Angels
Erika Langmuir
ISBN 978 1 85709 484 8

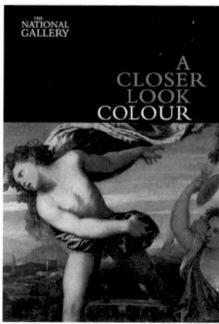

Colour
David Bomford and Ashok Roy
ISBN 978 1 85709 442 8

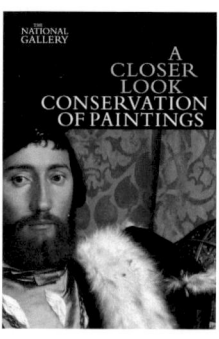

Conservation of Paintings
David Bomford with Jill Dunkerton
and Martin Wyld
ISBN 978 1 85709 441 1

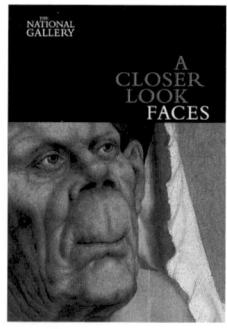

Faces
Alexander Sturgis
ISBN 978 1 85709 464 0

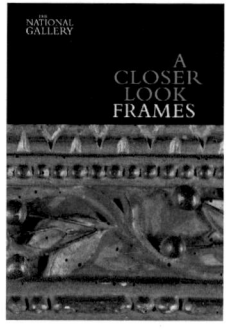

Frames
Nicholas Penny
ISBN 978 1 85709 440 4

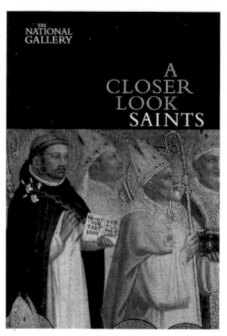

Saints
Erika Langmuir
ISBN 978 1 85709 465 7

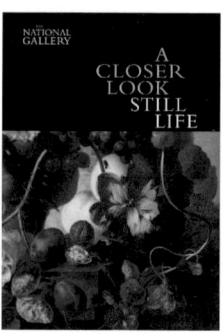

Still Life
Erika Langmuir
ISBN 978 1 85709 500 5

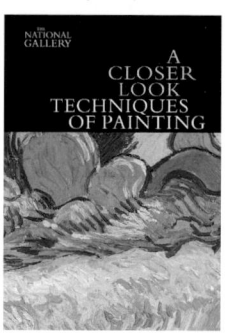

Techniques of Painting
Jo Kirby
ISBN 978 1 85709 534 0

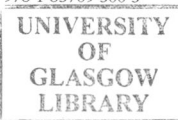